YESNO
DESIGN

"He brought me to the banqueting house, and his banner over me was love."

—Song of Solomon

My mother Ethel Stewart brought me to the

banqueting house, filling me with a love of art and

beauty. Over me was her all embracing love

and ceaseless encouragement, instilling in me the

confidence to pursue my highest ideals. No more

profound love did any mother show her child.

DIANE LOVE

YESNO DESIGN

Discover Your Decorating Style with
Taste-Revealing Exercises and Examples

Photography by Diane Love
and Christian Sarramon

RIZZOLI NEW YORK

CONTENTS

PART II: METHODS
EXERCISE YOUR TASTE

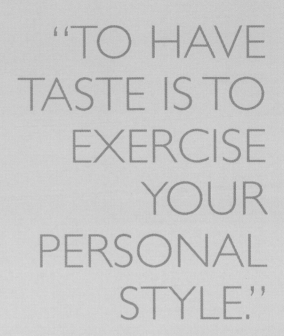

"TO HAVE TASTE IS TO EXERCISE YOUR PERSONAL STYLE."

INSTINCT AND ENCOURAGEMENT

These photographs of my former store and my New York apartment illustrate the way I like to arrange objects and furniture. They also reflect my partiality towards spaces with simple backgrounds against which the shape of the object and furniture is emphasized, as you can see with the procession of vases on the mantle shelf (opposite, upper left). Flowers are also an important element of the decor whether they are in a vase or a painting.

You are born with your own unique taste and sense of design. Your home is a sanctuary and its design should nurture you and be an expression of your taste. Most people feel to decorate a home successfully they must emulate the work of a well-known designer; they don't trust themselves to come up with a successful decoration. Professional designers have been encouraged, from an early age, to use their creativity and develop their skills; they are accustomed to trusting their intuition.

I am writing this book for the people who have been discouraged from expressing their creativity and so defer to designers and style setters. It's true, there are many talented designers writing books and being published in magazines, and their taste is wonderful, but it is not necessarily yours. Remember, you have to live with the decorating decisions made in your home, so those decisions should reflect your taste.

I grew up learning how to decorate. My playthings were fabric swatches and wallpaper samples. Antique stores, fabric showrooms, and wallpaper houses were my playgrounds. We moved nine times while I was growing up. Our homes were like set designs; with each apartment my mother created a new style of decoration. One home was a Moorish oasis of fretted window screens, glass mosaic floors, and a long banquette with loose cushions—it could have been out of *A Thousand and One Nights*. Another home was a "Venetian palazzo," whereby my mother had so successfully transformed her prosaic four-room New York apartment I was sure I could hear the water lapping against the gondolas.

My mother loved being original and trusted her own instincts and sense of design. Although I was dazzled by what she did, I discovered my taste was quite different from hers when I decorated my first home. As I grew to trust my taste more, the results were more satisfying because they were a reflection of who I was. I was fortunate to have been encouraged early to be creative, but there are no time limits on self-expression. Take the time now, for the reward is in the doing.

For twenty years I had a business and shop, Diane Love, Inc. on Madison Avenue in New York City. The shop grew out of my need for self-expression. Among the objects I sold were some of my creations—silk flowers, home accessories, dinnerware, jewelry, home fragrance, evening bags—and a choice of antiques. This was an unexpected mixture of goods, but the store was the product of my taste and everything I loved. Perhaps the shop should have been called Diane's loves!

Meeting people who responded to my designs and wanted to buy them was thrilling and encouraged me to take on even more ambitious projects. Getting to know these people was another unanticipated pleasure. However, I was always amazed at how many of them thought they were unclear about their taste—unsure what it

At first glance, the opulent decoration of my mother's former living room (opposite) appears to be in stark contrast to the studio/living room (above) I have in my country house, but they actually have many things in common. Both rooms have soft, dusty colors, subtly patterned fabrics, a meticulous placement of objects, and no window treatments. There is also much that is different. My mother had gilded furniture with curved lines, whereas my furniture is made of unembellished wood and has straight lines. Her living room was closed and private, while mine is bright and open.

was, unable to describe it, and unwilling to trust it. But it was no surprise to me they had no problem responding to the things they liked in the shop, since everyone has taste, and they express it instinctively all the time. It is just that most people have never been encouraged to identify, understand, and build on their taste. Consequently, they aren't confident about their taste and don't develop it.

Hoping to encourage this self-discovery, I created a questionnaire for customers to help them identify their likes and dislikes, which I thought would enable them put this knowledge to work when decorating their homes. The exercises and methods in this book expand on the concepts of that early questionnaire.

The key in learning how to decorate is to understand and identify your instinctive taste, trust it, and then learn how to apply it to create the decoration you want. This book provides the method to do this. You can create *your* decorating style.

There is nothing mysterious about decorating. The key to doing so is simple: you must learn what your taste is—to identify its characteristics, that is, your sense of balance, color, and arrangement. You also need to identify what type of atmosphere, architecture, furniture design, accessories, and fabrics you like and those you don't. At first you may think it is only important to know what you like, but knowing what you dislike is equally important. The challenge in decorating is to select from the thousands of design ideas flooding the marketplace the ones that are right for you. Once you are clear about your likes and dislikes, you will be decorating your way.

This book presents a step-by-step approach to your decorating self-discovery. The exercises here are simple and do not require any previous experience in decorating. The most important ingredient you can bring to these exercises is self-trust and the freedom of self-expression. I hope you enjoy and benefit from this book.

In my shop (below) the walls were painted taupe, then spattered with cream, pink, and mauve paint, a treatment that made the wall color subtle and versatile. The ceiling was covered with a dull silver paper, and the floor with mottled, faux-stone tile. Displays of merchandise were precisely arranged with a few objects and one of my silk flower arrangements. The cabinets below the displays made access to other objects easy. Both my shop and apartment (opposite) make clear my partiality for uncluttered spaces, bare floors, functional lighting, and dramatic furniture shapes.

EXERCISES

WHAT IS

"Whatever you can do, or dream you can, begin it; boldness has genius, power, and magic in it."
—Goethe

Everyone is born with his or her own taste: the more you exercise it, the better it develops. So use your taste creatively whenever you have the chance, whether you are dressing, entertaining, working, or decorating. Only you know what you really love, what inspires you, and what makes you feel good.

DON'T QUESTION YOUR TASTE.

And don't try to conform to anyone else's. Dancer and choreographer Martha Graham put it well: "Because there is only one of you in all of time, [your] expression is unique. And if you block it...it will be lost. The world will not have it. It is not your business to determine how good it is nor how valuable nor how it compares with other expressions. It is your business to keep it yours clearly and directly, to keep the channel open."

YOUR TASTE ?

THERE IS NO NEUTRAL SITUATION.

Whether you're conscious of it or not, you are constantly responding to what is around you. You react on some level to whatever you see, be it that empty hallway, your friend's leather sofa, the windows in your office, or the wallpaper at your local restaurant.

TASTE CAN NOT BE TAUGHT.

But it can be developed: we all need instruction and guidance to develop and learn. When you go to a museum or gallery you don't need anyone to tell you what you like and what you don't. You respond instinctively. I was reminded of this when I went to the Philadelphia Museum of Art with my friend Barbara and her three daughters, ages five to eight. Each of us had our favorite painting, and when we went to the museum's gift shop, each of us knew exactly which postcards we wanted to buy.

Some time ago, my husband and I visited an exhibition of the Danish artist, Hammershöi, at the Musée d'Orsay in Paris. He is an artist who did many depictions of the interior of his home; since I first discovered his paintings I have been intrigued by his spare gray rooms. I like their stillness and air of mystery, while my husband finds them melancholy and disquieting. As they say, "To each his own."

EXERCISE

1

EXPRESS YOUR IMPRESSIONS

Every decoration is a fusion of light, color, shape, space, and scale. The combination of these characteristics is what prompts your response to a room's decor. These four rooms (opposite) have been selected because they are very different from one another. None of them may have any relation to your taste, but by expressing your impressions of these rooms, you can begin to define your personal decorating style.

Y ou can't decorate your way unless you allow yourself to react freely to what you see. Exercise 1 encourages you to do just that, to feel comfortable with your own impressions. In this exercise, you are going to express your feelings simply and directly—trusting your responses and stating them as plainly as you can: your impressions.

Finding words to express your emotional reaction to what you see is amazingly helpful in pinpointing your impressions. Once you find those words, attitudes and reactions will come to the surface you never knew you had. An awareness of these feelings is enormously useful when decorating your way.

One of the qualities that is most appealing about a successful theatrical performance is the directness and strength of the actor's embrace of the character. The actor makes strong choices in order to communicate the character he or she is playing. Be an actor and make daring, dramatic choices when you select words to express your emotional response to what you see.

EXERCISE

1] Read the descriptive words on the opposite page. They are meant to evoke a strong response in you. Some of the adjectives may seem slightly repetitive: this is intended, as I want you to be able to choose words that reflect most accurately your way of describing what you see. Remember, there is absolutely no judgment attached to any of the words. I have selected them because they trigger strong feelings and describe numerous types of interior decoration.

calm	bare
comfortable	pretentious
sedate	cluttered
utilitarian	commonplace
open	cozy
lavish	dreamy
sparse	picturesque
crowded	uncontrived
stark	gaudy
opulent	flamboyant
poetic	romantic
extravagant	bold
busy	unpretentious

friendly	impersonal	regimented	modest
bucolic	spacious	sporty	informal
intimate	formal	grandiose	plain
stylized	casual	serious	refined
eclectic	palatial	predictable	severe
welcoming	exotic	bizarre	homey
fanciful	traditional	bland	grand
charming	theatrical	thematic	austere
elegant	bohemian	orderly	sleek
whimsical	impressive	empty	simple
hospitable	aggressive	spacious	airy
antiseptic	crowded	chic	sophisticated
forbidding	classic	overwhelming	stately

2] Look at the rooms shown here. Find three words on the list on the preceding pages that best express your reaction to each room.

3] Write the words that you have chosen on self-adhesive, removable note paper and stick it on the photograph. My impressions are in the caption below.

These rooms illustrate six diverse ways of decorating an interior. Each room is a personal creation. The words I have chosen define my reaction to each room. They are, no doubt, different from yours.

6) charming, intimate, modest
5) stylized, regimented, fanciful
4) stately, formal, classic
3) romantic, uncontrived, airy
2) theatrical, conspicuous, orderly
1) spacious, sophisticated, casual

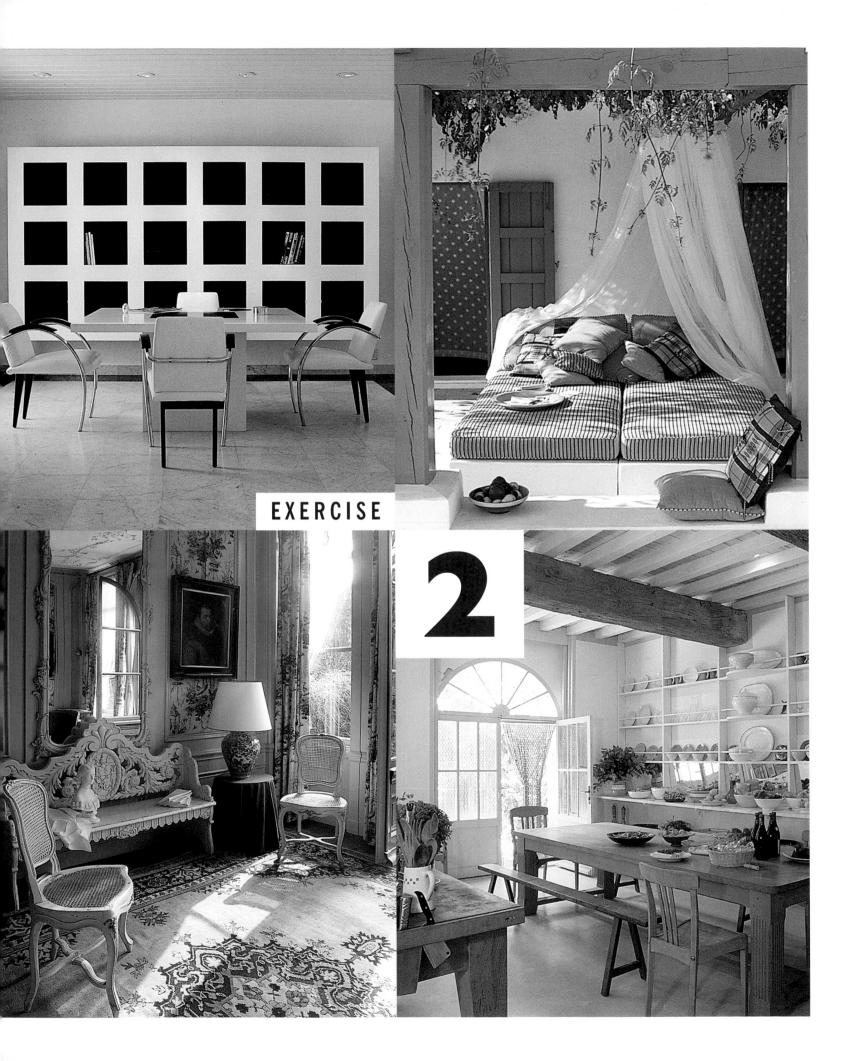

EXERCISE

2

LISTEN TO YOUR INTUITION

One of my favorite games when I was little was to look at pictures of rooms in magazines with my mother and tell her which I liked and which I didn't. It seems a very benign activity when I think back on it now, but it was such wonderful visual training for me.

For the moment, go back to doing things the way you did when you were a child. Remember how uncomplicated everything was; you knew what you loved and what you didn't, and you didn't censor your opinions. You had favorite clothes and favorite toys. Today you are still just as opinionated, but are probably more polite and don't blurt out your opinions. Exercise 2 is based on stating what you like and what you don't; it requires you to drop your self-restraint. Treat the exercise with a childlike freedom and lack of inhibition: you will get much more accurate and useful information.

The first tools you will need are a varied selection of home-decorating magazines. These magazines are filled with hundreds of decorating styles. You can make them valuable resources when you learn how to interpret your reactions to the photographs you see. Your reactions are the key to developing and establishing your decorating style.

Two people, Jeanne and Helen, did the exercises in this section. Each chose nine interiors that she liked and nine that she did not. These photographs (opposite) reveal part of their selection, analyzed in detail on the following pages. The reasons that motivated their choices are, without a doubt, very different but they both reacted strongly to the rooms they chose. Their individual personalities—and tastes—are expressed in their choices.

2

JEANNE'S TEST

] Leaf through some home-decorating magazines and tear or cut out nine pictures of rooms you really like. If you find yourself struggling over a photograph, wondering whether you like it or not, move on. If you felt strongly about it, you'd know. Don't second-guess yourself. It's also critical that you ignore any inclination you might have to be influenced by today's trends, fashions, or fads: they have nothing to do with your taste. If you don't have enough magazines on hand to complete the exercise, get more (back issues will do). Keep going until you have found nine rooms that you really love. These are your YESs.

Remember, your choices don't have to have anything to do with how you live or how you want to live. For the moment, forget about practical concerns. This is not a test to see how practical and efficient you are. It doesn't matter if the room looks hard to clean, if the furniture seems uncomfortable, if you choose a chateau or a houseboat. The purpose of this exercise is to help you get in touch with your true taste. Give yourself permission to entertain any and every fantasy. The Finnish summer house? The jazz musician's flat? The palace in Jaipur? The ranch house in Montana? The apartment in Amsterdam? If you like it, tear or cut it out.

Jeanne's YESs demonstrate a preference for light, airy, orderly spaces with strong, contrasting forms. (1, 2, 3, 4) These rooms represent a careful selection of precisely placed objects. There are no extraneous things—everything has its place. The black-and-white color scheme emphasizes the exactness of the room's arrangement. (5, 6) In these two rooms, the common denominator is the metal bed frame. The bed's square canopy is like a black box, framing the room's contents and imposing an order. It is also interesting to note there are no traditional lighting fixtures with lamp shades. (7) This room is another example of Jeanne's preference for white walls with dark objects silhouetted against them. (8) In this still life, the sense of order is still very evident. The room also has an unusual palette: the colors are soft yet strong, and the objects are simple in shape and color. (9) This kitchen's universal attraction is due to the combination of the light flooding the space and the sense of hospitality evoked by the food on the harvest table and counter.

JEANNE'S « **YES** » CHOICES

1

2

3

4

5

6

7

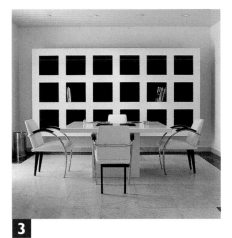

8

9

2] Take out your magazines and look at them again. In the same manner as step 1, cut or tear out nine pictures of rooms you don't like. These are your NOs. As with your YESs, be bold and choose the rooms that you truly dislike.

JEANNE'S TEST

Sometimes it's easier to understand a person's common denominators by first examining their NOs. In all cases but two (6, 9), Jeanne's NOs are rejections of traditional settings. She doesn't like spaces comprised of furniture with rounded shapes. In two cases (1, 7) the rooms have important chandeliers reminiscent of more traditional times. Rooms 2, 3, 6, 7, and 8 have oriental carpets and surfaces covered with objects, mirrors, statuary, and traditional paintings. (3) This office summarizes Jeanne's dislike of imposing, dignified settings: the Louis XV desk, with its papers and books, appears to await the attention of an official. (5, 6) A fire blazing in the hearth has long been considered a symbol of comfort and security in the home. Jeanne dislikes these rooms because they appear dark, stuffy, and airless. Most importantly, she rejects rooms with a warm, yellow glow, the characteristic common to all the rooms—and the exact opposite of the crisp, fresh, airy, angular rooms she selected as YESs.

JEANNE'S « **NO** » CHOICES

1

2

3

4

5

6

7

8

9

2

HELEN'S TEST

3] Now, look at your YES group, one picture at a time. For each room, write down your very first reaction about what you like in the picture on self-adhesive, removable note paper and stick it on the photograph. Don't think, just react. Your response might be very specific: you like the sofa, the color of the walls, the windows...or it might be emotional and more abstract: the room feels friendly, the space is elegant, the light is luminous.

4] Go through your NO responses and write down on self-adhesive, removable note paper what you don't like about each room you chose. It may be something specific or just a feeling. Does the room seem too crowded, too dark, too stark, too ornate, too flowery, too colorful, too cold? This will be easier to do than step 3, as we're usually more confident about identifying what we dislike than what we like.

(1, 2, 3) These rooms are all furnished and decorated in beige tones. The rooms look comfortable, with lots of places to sit and many green plants. (4, 5) These rooms have a studiolike feeling: private and highly personal, they both have stained wood surfaces that contrast with white walls. The strong diagonal of the staircase in room 5 and the diagonal line of the ceiling in room 6 suggest a preference for dramatic interior spaces with strong architectural elements. (6, 7, 8) These rooms are decorated in a soft blue-and-white color scheme. They are all simple, uncluttered sleeping areas. (7, 8, 9) These rooms underscore Helen's romantic partiality for sheer, gauzy fabric hangings over the beds. They look like sleeping areas you might find on an ideal vacation. (Actually, bedroom 6 is called "blue heaven" and it can be found at a wonderful bed and breakfast, Maison Garrance, which is situated in Saint-Saturnin-lès-Apt in Provence.)

HELEN'S «**YES**» CHOICES

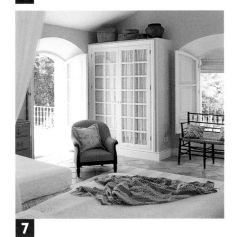

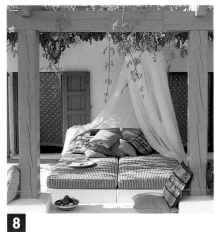

2

HELEN'S TEST

Since you are doing this exercise by evaluating photographs of other people's homes, it is important to keep in mind that your opinions are only important to you, not a reflection of the merits or flaws of a room's decoration or a criticism of another person's individuality and self-expression.

As you can see from the two examples presented in this exercise, each person's choices are inextricably linked to personal experience. After examining photographs of the same one hundred rooms, Jeanne and Helen came to very different conclusions. The only room they both liked was the airy kitchen with the open shelving and the only one they both rejected was the entrance space with its old-world elegance and formality. While Jeanne liked the bathroom for its orderly arrangement of objects, Helen disliked it. You see, there are no rights and wrongs in decorating.

(1, 2, 3) By choosing these rooms among her NOs, Helen confirms her rejection of decorations that are brash and intense in color. Red dominates each interior, and there is also an emphasis on patterned decorations—the very opposite of the serene blue-and-white rooms that attracted her. (4, 5) These two bathrooms are austere and precise, with not a sponge out of place. (6, 7) The rigid simplicity and meticulousness of the objects' arrangement exemplifies Helen's rejection of self-conscious order and this fresh almond green color. The hard, sleek surfaces and contrasting graphic patterns add to the feeling of anonymity and aloofness. (8, 9) With these choices, Helen again rejects rooms that feel formal and imposing—note the similar portraits and Louis XV side chairs.

HELEN'S «**NO**» CHOICES

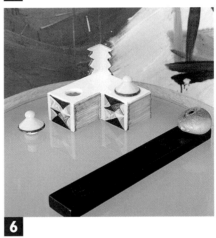

EXERCISE

3

IDENTIFY YOUR COMMON DENOMINATORS

They may look quite different, but these rooms (opposite) share common denominators. The person who chose the top two photographs, for example, prefers orderly, graphlike arrangements. (Top left) Note the symmetrical placement of furniture in this space: the wide blue-and-white striped sofa is set in front of the floor-to-ceiling mullioned window with its grid pattern of panes. All of these elements emphasize the regularity of the room's composition. This space (top right) demonstrates a preference for interiors laid out on a grid, which, in this case, is the checkerboard floor with all the furniture arranged at right angles on it. The mixed composition of pictures on the wall in this room (bottom left) and a similar asymmetrical composition of pictures in the kitchen (bottom right) suggest that the person who chose the two bottom photographs likes collections of sundry items arranged in a seemingly extemporaneous way, which creates a more relaxed setting.

No one asks you to explain why you are attracted to one thing and not to another, because it is human nature to react to feelings when making choices. Your taste is your way of selecting what you like from the things you experience. When decorating, you should avoid those things that make you react negatively.

Exercise 3 is going to help you identify those things that you respond strongly to. Do you already know what they are? Without a doubt, you do know some of them, but there are many more buried in your subconscious. Everything in your life—education, environment, culture, tradition, travel, and so on—goes to filling the reservoir of your intuitive responses. When I was eight years old my family spent some time in Europe as well as five months driving through forty-five of the then forty-eight states. We visited national parks, slept in countless motels, picnicked, ate in diners and restaurants, meandered down roads off the beaten track, and sped along highways bisecting vast fields of grain, corn, and cotton. Although I cannot quantify the results of these experiences, I know they have affected my sensibilities profoundly and are the key to the formation of my taste and style. What are your experiences and what is their impact on you? As you trace your common denominators you will come to understand your taste better.

In this exercise, you are going to identify the common denominators in the rooms you chose in Exercise 2. You are going to analyze your taste: a complex combination of feelings, experiences, and associations.

In order to tune into your unique taste, you must be able to step back from yourself and examine your YES/NO selections objectively. Only then can you determine the common denominators that appear in your selections. Objectivity is perhaps the most difficult requirement in doing this exercise, and is as hard for the professional to maintain as it is for the novice. Sometimes the thoughts that occur to you when you see something for the first time are the most true and unencumbered—be alert to these intuitions and make note of them. You can always abandon them later on if you decide they are not valid.

With this exercise, I discovered my husband's most important common denominators: comfortable, upholstered, sunny, light, and soft. Every room he liked was sunny and pale, and had large, upholstered seating. Once I understood this about him it made perfect sense to me that his favorite places in our homes are the sunny porch at our country house, the well-cushioned club chair in his home office, and the upholstered sofa in my studio. I, on the other hand, always sit in the straight-back wooden chairs.

In the process of writing this book I had the opportunity to analyze the tests of two other people I didn't know.

The YESs of the first person looked so contradictory the first time I saw them I thought that some of the photographs had been mixed up with others. But when I spread them out in front of me, I saw their common denominators. This person responded time after time to rooms that had, as part of their design, plaids, stripes, squares, floor tiles in a checkerboard design, small windowpanes, wainscoting, brick work, ladderback chairs, and rectilinear furniture shapes. I thought about these forms abstractly and realized that all of these elements formed a grid.

The NO selections confirmed my theory. This person repeatedly disliked rooms with furniture on the diagonal or in an asymmetrical arrangement, as well as patterns that had a diamond shape or harlequin motif. This made sense because diamonds, diagonals, and asymmetry break the grid structure. When I later met this person, I learned that she is a talented mathematician who works with computers, work that relies on the grid.

AN ORDERED PERSONALITY?

« YES »

« NO »

1] Pick up your YES choices again and spread them out in front of you. Look at them closely and find the common denominators. If you're overwhelmed by the prospect of doing this, start simply. Look at the room's architecture, windows, and structural materials; then look at the colors, fabrics, lighting, furniture, and objects. What do the rooms in your YES pile have in common? Write this down.

2] Once you have broken down each room's decoration, go back and look at it again as a whole. Try to look at the room in a more abstract manner. Common denominators are not limited to a specific decorative style or color. They may be the way the room is assembled or lit, or in the textures used. You are searching for the threads that connect your choices. You are trying to define something intuitive. Use the words in Exercise 1 to help you: write down the common denominators of the rooms you've chosen.

3] If your YES responses still seem unrelated, you may be looking for the wrong connections. A person with an objective viewpoint might be helpful in this case: ask him or her to look at your photographs and point out any connections they have noticed. Be sure you are comfortable with their observations—that they ring true—before you accept them, as finding what you like is the priority here. Once you start to define your taste more clearly, you will second-guess yourself less.

4] Repeat steps 1–3 for your NO choices.

The YESs of the second person were less perplexing. This person responded to rooms that were uncontrived, comfortable, and informal, with lots of stained wood in contrast to light-colored walls. The rooms look relaxed, with an array of pictures staggered on the wall, throws, and subtle patterns.

The NOs were equally consistent. This person rejected bare, impersonal, formal arrangements with black-and-white color schemes. This person always chose interiors full of the cozy details of a casual, friendly space: pillows, pictures, warm colors, and an eclectic assortment of objects.

A SENTIMENTAL PERSONALITY?

« YES »

« NO »

One time I analyzed the NO choices of a woman who consistently rejected the color white, most notably rooms that were white. This seemed to me a surprising dislike, considering the popularity of white in interior design today. Why would a person have such an aversion to white? The idea then struck me that she must have spent a lot of time in hospitals. I was right: as a child, she was constantly in and out of the hospital.

Unlike this woman, I always choose white or light-colored walls because they make a room feel larger and airier. I've also discovered that my choice of white reflects my need for a feeling of space. When my husband and I were looking for a country house, we agreed that we preferred country to seaside, a rural area to a gentrified one, a hilly landscape to a flat one. Most importantly, we wanted a feeling of openness—expansive views of the surrounding terrain from the house; we did not want to be nestled in the woods. Our house in upstate New York is perched on a hilltop with panoramic views in all directions. We are surrounded by open space outside and all of the rooms are painted linen white inside.

The kind of landscape we seek to live in is connected to our most basic sense of safety and security, as each of us is looking to find a location that makes us feel peaceful and protected. Some find it under a sheltering canopy of trees in a wood or forest, others near the pounding waves of the sea, while still others like to perch on the steep side of a mountain. This is an important question to explore with your family when you are looking for a home outside an urban area.

This is a guest bedroom in rural Connecticut. The bed alcove and chairs are draped in fabric, giving the room a mysterious and exotic air. The monochromatic color scheme emphasizes the interesting combination of textures in the room. The chest and wall plaques are a composition of rectangles. The painted ceiling molding and border on the floor also play up the rectangular forms. The column is not structural but adds dignity and dimension to the space. The unified look of this bedroom gives one the impression that its decoration was effortless. In reality, its success is due to the confidence the owner had in his taste. The walls and floor are painted white, making this room look serene and fresh—a guest bedroom perfect for a restful sleep on a summer night.

EXERCISE

4

CHOOSE THE RIGHT FURNITURE

D ecorating a home without an understanding of basic furniture styles is a bit like trying to cook a gourmet meal and only having access to a convenience store for food. You can't cook creatively if you don't have herbs, spices, and an array of fresh food stuffs to choose from. Exercise 4 helps you make informed choices about furniture. It presents the styles of yesterday and today, describes them briefly, and lists the most note-worthy designers of each.

These selections are meant to expand your awareness of the shapes and styles of the past—they are by no means complete. I have selected the styles and designers that I believe are the most familiar and whose work has met the test of time. One aspect of furniture not generally discussed, although an important part of its character, is its tactile quality. The styles I have listed have different tactile characteristics which you should keep in mind. There are many fascinating books on furniture design on the market today that can provide more in-depth information.

The purpose of this exercise is to put you at ease with the terminology used to describe furniture so that you will be able to select the furniture that corresponds to your taste. This will enable you to think of furniture in terms of its design profile and decorative details, not its pedigree.

All design is a product of its time. Furniture designs, like fashion designs, travel across borders and oceans. So while hemlines go up and down and silhouettes go in and out, furniture fluctuates in shape from curved to straight and back again.

The best way to understand furniture design, whether it's in the style of Art Deco, Louis XV, or in the styles conceived by Frank Lloyd Wright and Le Corbusier, is to understand its basic shape. When you see someone at a distance you see their silhouette first; as they come closer, you begin to notice their features. You can approach furniture design in the same way. First, look at the design profile of a chair: is it stocky, slim, tapered, elongated, thick, narrow? Then look at the decorative details that complete the style—the material (wood, metal, leather, plastic), ornamental features, and techniques (carving, inlay, joinery, and so on). The combination of the design profile and decorative details are what identify a furniture style.

This exercise is far from being an exact science. I have chosen several chairs to illustrate some of the most influential furniture designs in Western history and divided them into two groups: those with curved silhouettes and those with straight. This is a great oversimplification, but it provides a simple approach to getting acquainted with basic furniture designs. The name of the style is secondary; what is important is for you to identify the silhouette you prefer. (As a footnote, much furniture combines straight and curved silhouettes; when this occurs, I defer to the style that dominates the chair shown.)

As you go through the process of understanding furniture design, keep in mind your purpose, which is to be sure about what is right for your home. Before entering a store, be prepared and know what you're looking for. Listen to the suggestions of a salesperson if this is helpful, but don't get side-tracked: this is the time to exercise your taste!

This suite of Bentwood chairs (top) is enhanced by the pattern of the upholstery fabric, which echoes the soft, rounded lines of the furniture. These three utilitarian, low-back Shaker dining chairs (middle) are noteworthy for their simplicity, practicality, and excellent craftsmanship. The wavelike form of Mies van der Rohe's well-known tubular chrome armchair is a celebrated example of Bauhaus design.

EXERCISE

4

1] Examine the photographs of chairs on the next two pages. Make note of the shapes you like. Do you prefer a curved or straight silhouette?

2] Read the captions to identify which chair styles you like. Make note of the names of these styles.

3] Refer to pages 44–45 to read about the characteristics of the styles you have selected. Write down the specific decorative details you like.

ADAMS

AMERICAN COLONIAL

ARTS & CRAFTS

ART DECO

VICTORIAN

BEIDERMEIER

DANISH MODERN

EMPIRE

LOUIS XVI

NEOCLASSICAL

REGENCY

SHAKER

CURVED SILHOUETTE

ART NOUVEAU   CHIPPENDALE   LOUIS XV

QUEEN ANNE   MODERN   POSTMODERN

RENAISSANCE   BENTWOOD   BAUHAUS

ADAMS
18th century

This neoclassical British style went first to France, then to the United States. The polished mahogany chair pictured here illustrates this style's typical use of Grecian and Roman motifs such as swags, urns, and garlands. Its straight, tapering legs end in spade feet, reinforcing the delicate, formal characteristics of this type of design.

VICTORIAN
1837–1901

Victorian furniture is distinguished by its massive, weighty appearance. This dark mahogany chair is elaborately carved, and its stylized arches give the chair a lofty bearing. This chair has straight legs, but heavy curved shapes are also typical of the style.

LOUIS XVI
1750–1770

The straight fluted legs of this chair are typical of this formal style. Its ornamental flourishes are more studied and stiff, such as the stylized ribbon bow knot on the apron of the chair. This classic style is also characterized by subtle, geometric marquetry. Louis XVI furniture maintains a serious posture, unlike the more exuberant Louis XV.

AMERICAN COLONIAL
1600–1899

This chair is a good example of the simple, sturdy design of colonial American furniture. The turned stretchers look like sausages, while the side supports of the back have more graceful turnings with finials. The banister back and scalloped rail across the top give the chair a naive formality. The seat is made of rush, a commonplace material.

BIEDERMEIER
1820–1850

Biedermeier is distinguished by striking blond, satiny veneers with contrasting black details. The chair pictured here is a modest example of the lack of pretension with which this style marries different woods. The absence of carving is another characteristic of this northern European style.

NEOCLASSICAL
1750–1800

This imposing mahogany chair with parcel gilt embellishing the carved elements is characteristic of the dignified nature of Neoclassical style. The motifs (dolphins, feathers, paws) are all inspired by classical Greek and Roman furniture.

ARTS & CRAFTS
1870–1914

This handcrafted oak chair designed by Gustav Stickley combines stability and grace. Its erect posture and unembellished design make it look austere. The craftsman's high regard for joinery is visible in the finely made spindles and the overall fabrication of the chair. Gustav Stickley, Frank Lloyd Wright, and William Morris were the leading designers of this style.

DANISH MODERN
1940–1950

This armchair by Hans Wegner is an elegant example of the satiny, rounded forms that typify modern Danish design. The single-piece back rail curves around to make the arm rests and was inspired by Chinese chair design. The fine, unadorned hard wood is tactile as a smooth river stone. Hans Wegner, Arne Jacobsen, and Finn Juhl are the most noteworthy designers of this style.

REGENCY
1790–1840

This modest Regency chair has a shape reminiscent of early Greek chairs. The tapering, turned legs and back are enhanced with paint and gilt. This style has a formal quality, an influence of late Neoclassical design and a desired characteristic at this time in England.

ART DECO
1918–1939

The aerodynamic line of this three-legged chair by Emile-Jacques Ruhlmann reflects the growth of industrial design. The unbroken smooth surface of the pickled oak combined with the sleek green-leather upholstery are typical of the use of contrasting materials beloved by Art Deco designers. The style originated in France, but quickly gained popularity around the world.

EMPIRE
1804–1815

This chair reflects the monumental feeling of furniture created during Napoleon I's empire. The stately, square backrest and carved caryatid heads are intended to remind us of the victorious conquests of ancient Rome. The tapering legs end in a lionlike paw. These carved details are embellished with parcel gilt to make them even more regal.

SHAKER
1774–1810

This low-back dining chair is characterized by its lack of ornamentation and its practicality. Spare, clean lines and exceptional craftsmanship have made Shaker style admired the world over.

CURVED SILHOUETTE

ART NOUVEAU
1880–1914

This chair is one in a set of dining chairs designed by Louis Majorelle. The attenuated shapes are typical of this style as are the stylized flowers and foliage carved into the wood. Principal designers of this style include Hector Guimard, Louis Majorelle, Carlo Bugatti, and Antonio Gaudi.

QUEEN ANNE
1702–1714

The graceful shape of this needlepoint wing armchair with cabriole legs ending in paw feet is a classic example of this type of design. The cabriole leg of this style is more restrained in shape than that of the Louis XV, as it is stiffer with thicker ankles and heavier knees.

RENAISSANCE
15th–16th centuries

The X chair, also known as a Savonarola chair, is Italian in origin. It is a wonderful example of practical construction. The use of dark wood accentuates its imaginative shape.

CHIPPENDALE
18th century

This mahogany chair illustrates American Chippendale at its best. It includes several of the style's most recognizable features: a carved back-splat and rail (which on this chair is a lyrical composition of loops and curves), prominent knees, and ball-and-claw feet. The seat covering, although not original, is also typical of the flame-stitch patterns used at the time.

MODERN
1920–1950

This functional chair, with its clean lines, is characterized by its lack of ornamentation and by its striking use of molded plywood. Leather, steel, and plastic were also popular materials. Alvar Aalto, Charles Eames, Gerrit Rietveld, and Le Corbusier were the key designers of this style.

BENTWOOD
1830–1910

Rounded forms, curves, and spirals are characteristic of this distinctive style. Michael Thonet invented the process by which solid lengths of wood could be steamed or boiled to make them pliable, a manufacturing procedure that was used in the construction of this armchair.

LOUIS XV
18th century

This beechwood armchair, with its upholstered back and arms, captures the lyrical, undulating quality of this style. The curvaceous shape of the cabriole leg is accentuated by the way it is carved; this distinctive swelling curve is the most defining feature of the style. The arms and cartouche-shaped back echo the serpentine undulation; carved floral motifs, also characteristic, provide an additional playful flourish.

POSTMODERN
Since 1960

This molded plastic chair by Steen Ostergaard is a fine example of an inventive application of modern technology. Sculptural in form, the chair is of one piece and is stackable, reflecting the contemporary need to make the most of space.

BAUHAUS
1918–1933

The Bauhaus designers employed the new manufacturing tech-nologies of their time to create beautiful, fluid shapes out of tubular steel. Their materials were machine-made, but their designs were inspired by their dedication to aesthetics. Walter Gropius, Marcel Breuer, and Mies van der Rohe were the top industrial designers of the day.

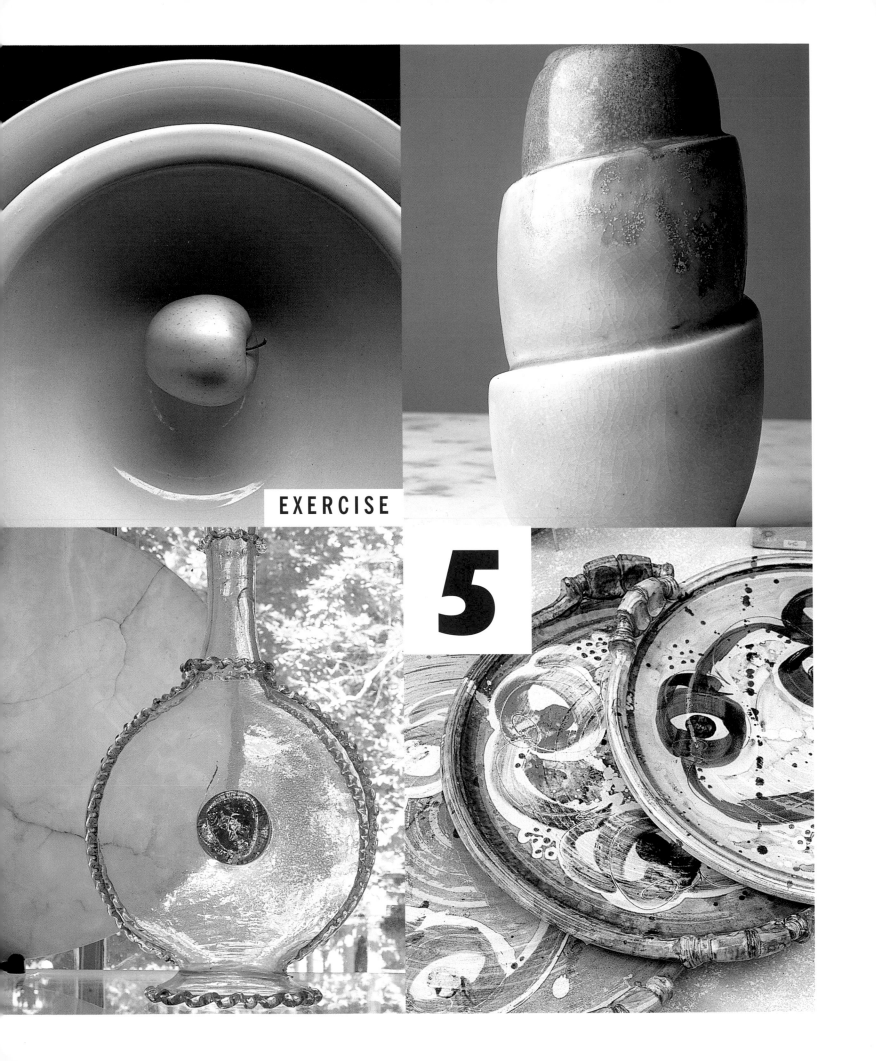

EXERCISE

5

SELECT DECORATIVE OBJECTS

The expression "It just caught my eye" is very accurate. Wherever you go—a store, a friend's home, an antiques show, a museum—your eye functions in the same way. It scans everything and alights on the things it finds most interesting, beautiful, ugly, weird, unique, novel, or familiar...all the rest is extraneous and is virtually edited out. Exercise 5 is going to help you understand what catches your eye. It explores the world of objects to identify those you like and those you don't.

What do we mean by objects? For the purpose of this discussion, I've divided objects into two groups: large and small. Large objects are chairs, cabinets, sofas, desks, chests, tables, sculptures, tapestries, murals, paintings, rugs, appliances, and so on. Small objects are accessories, the things you put on top of large objects or on the wall such as pictures, pillows, lamps, books, dishes, clocks, and quilts. Small objects can be as mundane as kitchen dishes, as functional as a computer, as unique as a drawing, or as decorative as a vase of flowers. Whether large, medium, or small in size, functional or decorative, rare or common, an object can be looked at abstractly, as a composition of form, color, pattern, and texture.

Form, color, pattern, texture: identifying objects by their main characteristic enables you to describe more easily and define more clearly what catches your eye. These commonplace bowls are striking because of their unusual color (opposite, top left). The controlled coiled form of this small vase makes it distinctive (top right). The frill of glass adorning this hand-blown Venetian decanter adds interest to its texture (bottom left). The flourishing brush strokes, loose and extemporaneous, create a bold pattern on these platters (bottom right).

I have a friend with glorious red hair. She has other very attractive features as well, but if I were describing her to a stranger who was to meet her on a crowded street corner, I would tell them to look for my friend's red hair because it is her most distinctive characteristic. It is the same with objects; they, too, have one characteristic that is more eye-catching than another.

Sometimes the most distinguishing thing about an object is its form, as is the case with a grand piano or an umbrella. Sometimes an object's form is commonplace and its most striking feature is its color, as exemplified by a clover-purple bowl, a persimmon pillow, or a radish-red sugar shaker. Pattern can be a distinguishing feature, too. A chessboard without its squares could be a bread board, a patchwork quilt, a plain cover. There are all kinds of patterns—figurative, floral, geometric, and free-from. Finally, texture is the most difficult characteristic to define, but no less important, and applies to the material the object is made of. Take, for example, a silver teapot, a glass decanter, a woven basket—in each case it is the texture of the material that makes each object distinctive.

Start identifying objects using these four basic definitions: you'll find it gives you a simple way to categorize what you see and pinpoint what caught your eye in the first place.

Form (opposite) is one of the principal characteristics of an object, be it geometric, figurative, or organic.

Page 50: These utilitarian objects are made special by their color. The lavender and banana colors of these bowls are offbeat and interesting in combination (top left). The two "jadeite" cups are a luminous lettuce green (top right). This radish-red sugar shaker (bottom left) is great to use when serving berries. The colors of the wash basin and pitcher (bottom right) would be the perfect complement to a big bunch of lilacs.

Page 51: These commonplace shapes are characterized by their patterns, be they abstract, geometric, or representational. Splashes and drips swirling on these platters make for a very energetic pattern (top left). The bold black strokes on this vase appear to be abstractions of the human form (top right). The sponge pattern on the mixing bowl (bottom left) is what distinguishes it as a decorative object, while the snow-laden pine on this Japanese vase tells a poetic story (bottom right).

FORM

COLOR

PATTERN

TEXTURE

EXERCISE 5

1] Look through the magazines you were using for Exercise 2 or, if you like, begin with a new group. Now find objects in the rooms that attract you, bearing in mind the discussion of form, color, pattern, and texture on pages 47–48. Do not confine yourself to the pictures you used for your YES responses in Exercise 2, as there may be an object you like in a photograph that you did not choose. Circle the objects you like, and put those pages aside.

A texture can be translucent, reflective, rough, or fibrous. The Venetian glass decanter (opposite, top left) diffuses the light, while the etched silver tea set glistens with reflections (top right). The home-spun earthenware pitcher is dull (bottom left), and the woven basket (bottom right), a network of flat and round fibers.

2] Now look at the objects you circled and decide which of its characteristics is most important. Look at the object in terms of the feature which caught your eye. Is it the shape of the rocking chair, the yellow paint on the armoire, the marquetry of the writing table, the shininess of the chrome coffee table? Sometimes it is hard to decide on the most important characteristic. An object may have two characteristics of equal importance, such as a beautifully veined marble statue (texture and shape); a lustrous pomegranate velvet bedspread (color and texture); an impeccable handwoven Shaker blanket with a geometric border (texture and pattern); and a colorful English ironstone platter with a floral pattern (color and pattern). When this occurs in your evaluation of an object, write down both characteristics because it will help you clarify what you are responding to. But don't choose more than two.

3] Look at the objects you've circled. Have you found consistencies in your choices? Have you discovered your preferences? Do you most often choose objects with a striking shape, unexpected color, dazzling surface pattern, or unusual texture? Make a list of the objects you have circled and identify each object with one of the four descriptive words.

EXERCISE

6

DEFINE YOUR COLOR PALETTE

Color is an essential part of our daily experience. At the market, we sort through the fruits and vegetables for the specimen with just the right color. We are attracted to the colors in the flower stall. We are moved by light reflecting off a stark white surface, stilled by the dark womblike feeling of black space. Dressing, too, is comprised of sorting, matching, and combining colors: but we are used to, and therefore comfortable with, these daily choices. When you use color in decorating, the principles are the same, but the scale is grander. When you decorate, you are working on a much larger area, so it's harder to visualize and experiment, and mistakes are much more costly.

The most important thing to remember about color is that it does not exist in isolation. A color takes on its identity when it is placed next to another color; Rothko, Turner, Matisse, van Gogh—the great colorist painters—all knew this.

You have learned a great deal about your taste. You have used words to describe your emotional reaction to a decoration, distinguished your likes from your dislikes, traced the connections running through your choices, and selected the furniture shapes and objects that attract you. The one aspect of decorating you have not focused on is color. In my opinion, color is the most important characteristic: it is the glue that holds everything together.

Color has a powerful emotional impact. That's why it is essential that the colors in your home comfort you and have lasting appeal. Don't be diverted by the color fad of the moment and give up what is best for you. It is the business of home furnishing companies to promote different colors each year to generate interest and excitement in their products. Sometimes these promotions open your eyes to a new color you like but they may also distract you.

What is your palette going to be? How do you choose from the vast array of colors available? What are the colors that nurture you and make you comfortable? How do you choose from the thousands of colors available? The more you can narrow down this selection, the easier it will be for you to make the right choice.

One way to narrow down the field is to describe what you want in terms that are readily understandable and easy to visualize. If, for example, you told someone you wanted to paint the shutters on your house a slightly "warm yellow," the likelihood of this person accurately visualizing your perception of this color is very slim. But if you told someone you wanted to paint your shutters a dandelion yellow, the visual picture of what you described is clear.

Another way to insure that you get the results you're striving for is to find actual finished examples of what you think you want. When my daughter Victoria moved with her family into a Victorian clapboard house, they wanted to repaint it, and my daughter was sure she wanted to repaint it yellow. But what color yellow? Sunflower, chamois, buttercup, lemon, banana? I suggested she try to describe the yellow she was visualizing in terms of objects with specific colors that we both could relate to. We ended up going through a list of yellow fruits and vegetables, and the fruit that came closest to what she had in mind was a grapefruit. Our next step was to drive around her neighborhood to see if we could find an example of something painted grapefruit yellow. Not too far from her home, we found what we were looking for. After seeing her color idea on another house, she was even more convinced that it was the right choice. There is no better way to confirm your ideas than finding a finished example of what you have in mind.

When you paint a room an intense color, it can immediately simplify other decorating decisions. The lapis lazuli color of this dressing room/study (opposite, top) envelops you in an atmosphere of grandeur and establishes the look of the space. All the upholstery matches the walls; the painting and prints are enhanced by the blue; the pears and emerald-green lamp shade stand out like jewels. This gracious spiral staircase (bottom) is in a foyer in Provence. The warm cinnamon-brown walls welcome the visitor, while the black iron railing and faux marble baseboards enhance the curved shape of the space without competing with the overall color. The only piece of furniture is a functional chair.

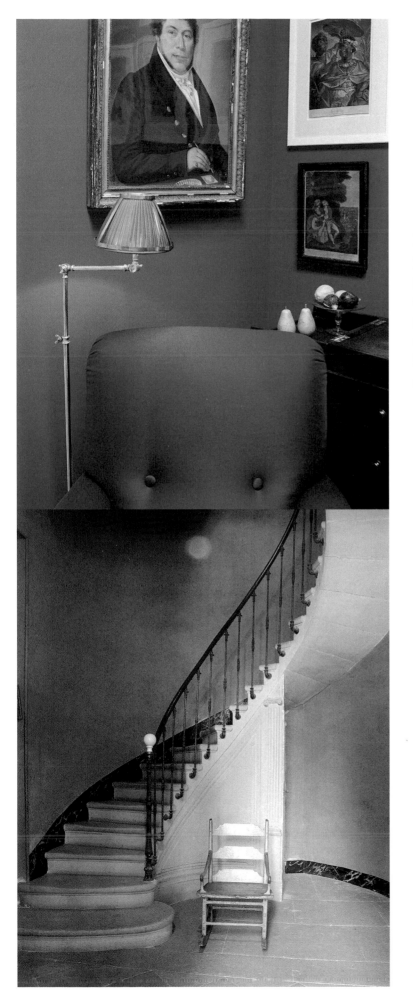

In Exercise 6, you'll determine the specific colors you like. On the following pages are lists and photographs of familiar objects with specific colors. Objects with specific colors are objects that are always the same color. A cornflower is always the same blue, whereas the sky and sea are blue, but the shades of blue are endless and change with the slightest shift of light, weather, or season.

EXERCISE

6

1] Look through the lists of fruits, vegetables, flowers, and objects on the following pages and make note of those whose colors please you.

2] Attach to these specific colors, and to any other specific colors you like, words to describe the characteristics you find attractive about the color. Is it pale, vivid, dull, intense, electric, faded, soft? It's important for you to be able to talk comfortably about your color preferences with those who are helping you implement your decoration. The ability to communicate your ideas precisely will save time and money, and help prevent disappointment.

GOLDEN DELICIOUS APPLE

BANANA

APRICOT

DANDELION

ZUCCHINI FLOWER

SUNFLOWER

CARROT

DRIED RAISINS

RED PURPLE

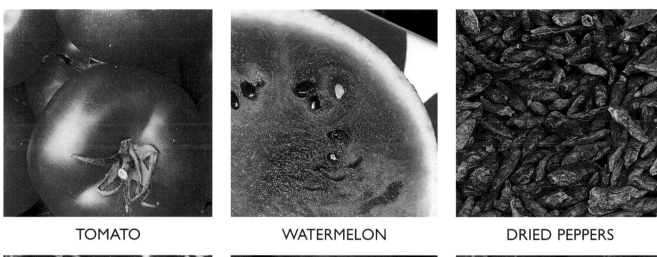

TOMATO   WATERMELON   DRIED PEPPERS

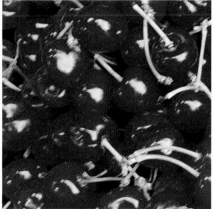
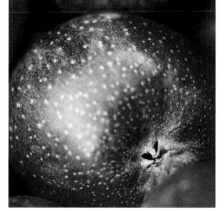

CHERRIES   APPLE   RASPBERRIES

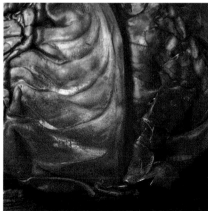

RED ONION   CABBAGE

?

BLUE VIOLET

TURQUOISE

PERIWINKLE

DELPHINIUM

GENTIAN

BLUEBERRIES

FORGET-ME-NOT

LAVENDER

EGGPLANT

?

GREEN

ARTICHOKE

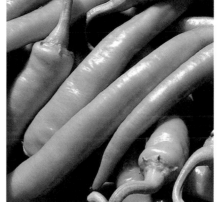

PEPPERS

FRESH ALMONDS

DILL

STRING BEANS

SCALLIONS

ZUCCHINI

CHARD

?

OCHER BROWN

POTATOES

MUSHROOMS

KIWI

PECANS

BOSC PEARS

SHALLOTS

ALMONDS

PAPRIKA

ONIONS

WHITE ROSE

DANDELION

EASTER LILY

BLACK RADISH

LICORICE

FIGS

BLACKBERRIES

EXERCISE

7

COMBINE COLORS

A combination of monochromatic colors gives this room (opposite, top left) a serene atmosphere. The sunlight sifted through the sheer curtains adds to the tranquil feeling. The chair and ottoman in the corner of this bedroom (top right) are covered in a large plaid fabric, the colors of which link the blue walls and saffron-colored window hangings. The orange door and neon-green walls of this dining area (bottom left) is a daring use of opposing colors. In this summer dining room (bottom right), the use of accenting color adds brightness and whimsy. The simple folding chairs have easily removable slipcovers for the back and loose, tie-on cushions for the seats, which permits the owner to combine the accenting colors in numerous ways.

The world of color is immense and spectacular. How do you choose from this vast array the colors that will nurture you and make you most comfortable? You have to know how to compare and evaluate them. Are they hot, cool, saturated, pale? Are they complementary or do they oppose each other?

Color is technical as well as emotional. When making choices, you have to think in terms of how the color you want to use relates to the other colors you are considering. Do the colors clash or blend? Do they brighten or dull each other? Is one color lighter or darker, or do they have the same degree of luminosity? To help you understand the ways colors combine, I've broken down color into four groups—monochromatic; relating, or linking; clashing, or opposing; and punctuating, or accenting—and discuss them in detail on the following pages.

Now is the perfect time to test and sample color combinations you may have secretly liked but never dared to use. You will find after you have experimented with these colors you'll better understand how they interact with other colors. Whatever you can do to expand your understanding of color relationships is beneficial and instructive.

A vestibule is a circulation space; using a monochromatic palette in a transitional area is one way for the eye to move seamlessly from one room to another. This vestibule uses a range of colors in the same tone—represented by the three vegetables shown here. The garlic is the same luminous white as the diaphanous curtains. The white eggplant matches the brilliant white of the sculpture, and the furniture relates to the color of the pecans, the darkest color in the setting.

CREATE SERENITY WITH A MONOCHROMATIC PALETTE

Some spaces have a very peaceful, restful feeling. This effect is often achieved through the use of monochromatic color. As a result, the eye floats easily over the surface of the room because there is no contrasting color to command its attention and stop it. Even an all-red room can be soothing if there is no contrasting color to jar the eye. Thus you can control the mood of your space by the amount of color contrast you create.

Captivated by the vibrant colors she saw on a trip to India, the owner of this bedroom draped its windows romantically with saris she bought there. The sapphire-blue walls, saffron-colored carpet, and red and purple saris come together in the spirited plaid fabric on the armchair and ottoman. The color of the apples and beets are the transition colors in this bedroom, linking the walls, saris, and carpet.

INTRODUCE A LINKING COLOR

Another method of working with colors is to link them, that is, to create color "bridges" that move the eye from one color to another color by means of an intermediary color.

When I did flower arranging in my shop I found a simple way to unify an arrangement was to link the colors. I would begin by choosing flowers representing the two most predominant colors. Then I would decide what color flower or foliage I needed to link these two colors together. I did this by imagining what color I would get if the flowers were paint and I could mix them together.

The same approach applies to decorating. Once you have selected your dominant colors, you need to determine what colors join them. This is an important concept to understand, even if you don't choose to decorate this way in your home, and it is very useful and easy to master.

Another way to link colors is to use wallpaper, fabric, or an object that includes both colors. In dressing, a scarf often serves this purpose. The colors aren't really mixed, of course, but the eye mixes them and creates the visual connection. French pointillist painters understood this concept very well. Georges Seurat, for example, placed thousands of dots of different colors side by side on the canvas, and the viewer's eye mixed them, creating a readable image.

The design of this eating area is dominated by its color scheme. The simple chairs and semicircular table blend into the color of the background. The sharp apple-yellow picture frame, the whimsical yellow straws, and the orange door all stand in opposition to the neon-green walls. This is a theatrical color scheme for a modest space.

USE OPPOSING COLORS

A third way to combine colors is to use colors that oppose each other, or clash, thus playing off of each other. This effect is produced most successfully when one color is warm and the other is cool. As an example, a tomato—an orange red, or warm color—clashes with a red cabbage—a blue red, or cool color.

When I was a teenager, it was the style when dressing formally to have your shoes dyed to match your dress. You went to the shoe store, dress in hand, to find the perfect match. I finally rejected this practice of "dyed to match" and decided to choose a shockingly different color—an opposing color—for my shoes. I once wore a pale peachy pink dress and accenting fuchsia-colored satin slippers—and I felt like Cinderella!

The furniture in this dining space is rustic, the plaster walls and ceiling painted a warm brown similar in color to the Bosc pears shown here. The chairs are covered in a variety of colors—a charming way to relieve monotony and introduce accenting colors. A string-bean green, a raspberry red, and a deep lapis-lazuli blue punctuate the line-up of chairs. The introduction of these accent colors gives the owner more colors to work with when selecting dinnerware and flowers for the centerpiece.

EXPERIMENT WITH ACCENT COLORS

This fourth method consists of introducing a more saturated color, that is, a color rich in pigment so that the color is deeper and more intense. Using color this way boosts the color impact of a room by playing off the colors in the room and bringing them into focus. Because accenting colors startle the eye, they make a room look brighter and livelier. Accenting colors are often introduced by a decorative object, although painting the room's trim an accenting color can be effective, too.

1] Go back to your answers in Exercise 2 and study the color concepts you liked. What was your preferred way of combining color? Monochromatic, linking, opposing, or accenting? If you don't have enough examples to determine your preference, look through more magazines and cut out the photographs of rooms where color is used in a way that appeals to you. Base your selections only on the way color has been used in the room; disregard everything else.

2] If you have selected more than one color concept, don't worry. You don't have to use the same color idea in every room. Determine what other color concepts attract you and find other photographs that represent them. Find as many examples as you can, because the more you research your ideas, the more confident you will be about applying them.

3] Some color concepts may be played out successfully in one type of room, but not in another. In your research you may have admired a kitchen with opposing colors, but do you want to use opposing colors to create such a lively effect in your bedroom? Look at all the photographs you have selected and compare the function of the room in the photograph with the function of the room you are going to decorate. Is the color concept used in a room of the same function? Will the color concept work as well in your room? Ask yourself these kinds of questions, bearing in mind that what looks great in one place may be completely unsuitable in another.

CONCLUSION

The essential ingredient to decorating successfully is enjoying the process—giving yourself over to the ideas that occur to you when you least expect them to. You cannot plan when you are going to have a creative thought, so you must be receptive to these ideas as they come to you. Don't hesitate when you have creative ideas—write them down immediately, as you don't want to lose these thoughts as fast as you get them. There are blank pages in the workbook included with the book that provide a space for you to do this.

The first part of this book asked you to cut through fads and fashions to discover your true taste. The exercises you have completed have given you permission to discover your creative potential and be receptive to new and unfamiliar ideas by learning to be observant and using every opportunity to expand your understanding. Now, are you beginning to understand your taste? If you feel uncertain, review your responses to the exercises and ask yourself if you did them with your heart or with your head. Let your heart lead the way, for a cerebral approach only leads to a dead end.

Your taste is the result of the alchemy of your life experience—family, education, socioeconomic background, environment, and many other factors. There is no way to analyze how these forces have influenced you exactly. What is certain is the way you have assimilated your experience is what makes you—and your way of expressing yourself—unique. It is essential to have confidence in your impressions and cherish your individuality.

The second part of this book dissects and explains the methods I have always followed when I decorate an interior. These methods demonstrate decorating in slow motion and can be applied to any decorating project, large or small. Today, I always follow the same procedures, even when I appear to work quickly, because each situation is different and can never be done automatically.

METHODS

EXERCISE

Interior decorating is much like assembling a giant jigsaw puzzle. The proper assembly of the various pieces forms the picture. From this point of view, the pieces create an interlocking design, and every element you add must fit and reinforce your decorating plan.

In general, there are three basic decorating scenarios:

YOU OWN NOTHING AND ARE MOVING INTO A NEW HOME.

You may be starting out with a brand new space and no furnishings—a truly blank canvas! What an exciting opportunity, to start from scratch. However, most people are often uncomfortable with empty rooms and rush to paint them and make purchases. Slow down, take advantage of the situation, and enjoy the emptiness. Before you acquire anything, be sure you understand your space (see Method 2, page 88) and have chosen a decorative focus (see Method 5, page 112).

YOUR TASTE

YOU ARE MOVING FROM ONE HOME TO ANOTHER.

In this case, rethink what you own and how you decorated your old home. Take time to create a plan that reflects the new space and your evolving taste. Even if the movers are hurrying you and you're anxious to get settled, resist the temptation to place furniture automatically—in the same way or much in the same way it was arranged in your old space.

YOU ARE PLANNING TO REDO YOUR EXISTING HOME.

Again, it is essential to start with a clean slate. To do this, remove every object and piece of furniture from the room in question into an adjacent space. This is very time consuming and inconvenient, but it is the only way to see the space clearly. If the walls are decorated or painted, imagine them blank. Redecorating is more than re-covering furniture and repainting walls; its purpose is to create a cohesive decorative design.

Decorating is analogous to the way a painter works. Like an artist, you begin with a blank canvas, that is, an empty room. Even if you plan to design every room in your house you must work as an artist does: canvas by canvas, or room by room. Begin with the room or connected spaces you consider most important. Like other art forms, decorating combines inspiration and technique. I have not yet met an artist who does not combine the two. The first part of this book focused on helping you find what inspires you and liberating your self-expression. Now, with the methods I've defined, you will learn how to express yourself through decorating concepts you like.

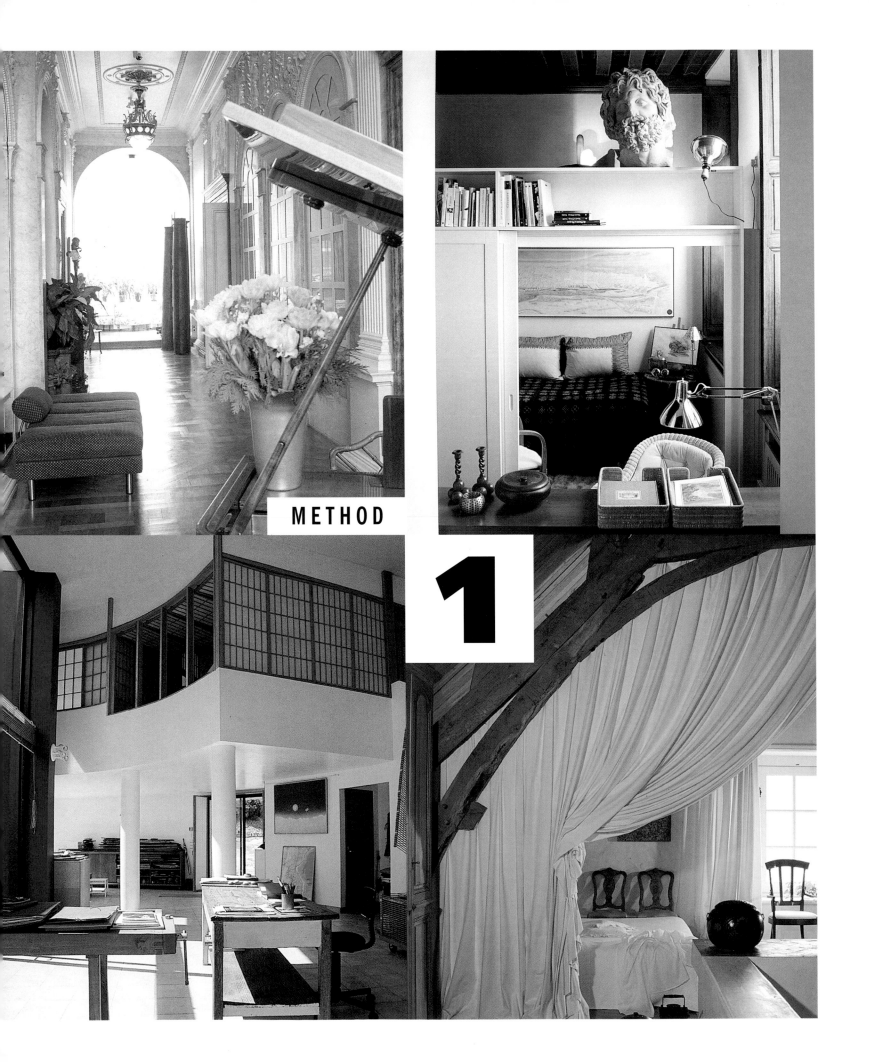

METHOD

1

USE SPACE EFFICIENTLY

The decoration of your home must allow for your activities there. It is in this wide hallway (opposite, top left) that the owner has chosen to locate a piano. The abundant light and uncluttered space allow a musician to practice privately or perform in front of a small gathering. This sleeping area (top right) is also an office. It has been divided by a partition just high enough to afford privacy to someone in the bedroom while another person works in the office area. The artist who built this studio (bottom left) for her print work tucked her bedroom behind moveable Japanese rice paper screens in the loft area overhanging the studio. The generously gathered drapery makes this sleeping area (bottom right) feel like a Bedouin tent—a serene retreat just beyond the work area.

As I see it, decorating is creating an aesthetic composition that is at once pleasing and practical. In this light, the first priority is to define the function of the room you are going to decorate. Years ago, when space was not at such a premium, many grand homes designated a room for a single activity. There were billiard rooms, ballrooms, morning rooms, and libraries. Today most of us don't have the luxury of extra space; we have to be resourceful and use our space at home in both an efficient and attractive way. Unless you know how a room is to be used you cannot decorate it successfully. In determining the function of a single room, you must also determine the function of all the other rooms. Light, noise, and location are critical considerations when choosing a room's function, too. Does the room get morning or afternoon light—or no direct light? Is it in a quiet or noisy location with regard to exterior traffic and activity? Is it tucked away in a basement, attic, or back area, or is it adjacent to an active area?

In most cases the architectural layout of a home makes the function apparent, but there are always exceptions. Since your needs and lifestyle are unique, you must tailor your home to suit you. You may see a space adjacent to the kitchen as ideal for eating and entertaining, but if you work at home you might prefer eating in the kitchen and using the adjacent space as an office. If you have young children, the space may be the perfect playroom so you can cook with the children in view.

ecorating has always required solving both the aesthetics and function of a space. Form always follows function. Our New York apartment is decorated around my daily routine of writing and painting, because I am the one who works at home. Our country house is used mostly on weekends, the time when my husband writes, so there, he has the spacious study. Our limited space also requires this same study to function as a guest room when friends stay overnight. My weekends are occupied with gardening, antiquing, photography, and small art projects. My favorite work area is our open kitchen, which has high ceilings. I work at our very spacious dining table from which I can look out on the flower garden. In winter I am warmed by the wood stove no matter how snowy the weather.

This open room (top) is the quintessential flexible space; all at-home activities occur within these four walls. My studio (bottom) is organized as efficiently as possible. Paintings are stored in the rack on the right of the mantle, works on paper in the flat files on the left.

METHOD

1

- Evaluate how you spend your time at home. Determine what is most important to you and don't be influenced by the lifestyle of anyone else. There are people who love to entertain and, even though it occupies only a fraction of their time at home, it is a priority—and their decoration reflects this function. What are your priorities? Some years ago my husband and I realized that we were spending too much time watching television in the evening before going to bed. At the time, the television was in our bedroom. We moved it to my husband's work area, and I was amazed how such a simple change could alter our lives. Now our television watching is much more selective. I read more before going to sleep, and our bedroom has become a tranquil oasis.

- Think about how you and your family spend time at home. If it helps, make a schedule of the activities that occur at your home over the course of a week.

- Walk through your empty home and designate the function of each of your rooms. Then ask yourself the following questions: What are my most important activities at home? What is my lifestyle—formal or casual? Am I a homebody, a socializer, a traveler? Is this room better for work or recreation? What rooms will I keep private? Public? Which rooms are better during the day? At night? Does the season affect the use of the room?

- Most spaces can be multipurpose; if this is the case, you must first define the room's most important function. If you have children, the needs of each member of the family need to be factored into your thinking.

METHOD

2

UNDERSTAND YOUR ARCHITECTURE

The architecture of this kitchen (opposite, top) combines brick, tiled, and plastered walls. The tall arched window and the high mantle shelf on the right both accentuate the height of the ceiling. The architecture of this bathroom (bottom) is very strong and enhances the traditional bathtub and pedestal sink. The angled ceiling, wainscoted walls, tub platform with its marble top, and the small square windows utilize a variety of structural materials and together create very interesting volumes and an architectural rhythm in this small, white, and wood-stained space.

Although we are all made in the same way, each of us possesses different physical characteristics that make us recognizable and give us individuality. We know our dimensions and our best features. You need to become as familiar with the parts of your home. The style, shape, and size of your space determine its personality and influence your choices for decorating it. More than likely, you chose your home because something about it appealed to you. What could be more important then for you to unite its architecture to your decoration?

Before decorating your home, you need to define its characteristics, determine its dimensions, and examine the architecture and the materials used in its construction. Also examine the size and shape of its rooms, and the arrangement and style of windows, doors, and other structural features. Old buildings usually have more information to analyze than modern ones.

But just because a space is new and has fewer architectural details does not mean it has less personality. As an example, while my husband and I were visiting southern France, we had the good fortune to meet a married couple who worked together as architects. They spoke passionately about architecture and about the home they were building for themselves just outside the small village where we were staying. One day we were invited to see their not-yet-finished house. It was small but majestically situated overlooking a gorge and mountain range. Its small size did not diminish the power and elegance of its shape. Every room inside reflected the simple geometry of the exterior.

To understand your space you must look at it as a whole. If you wish to add, change, or remove any architectural elements, now is the time to decide. You should only make alterations when you understand how your rooms relate architecturally.

The single most important thing to do when you first acquire a home is to remove whatever element conflicts with your decorating plan. It is imperative that all architectural changes be done before anything else, as architecture is the skeleton of a room, and its structure determines what follows. Keep in mind that just because something is architectural does not make it untouchable. Often homes have been altered by previous occupants, sometimes to the benefit of the space, sometimes not. Do not keep any architectural element just because it's there; examine your space carefully and determine which architectural elements are an asset and which should be eliminated. Of course, you can't remove an architectural element without first determining if it is structural, hence necessary to support the building!

My first country house was a gardener's cottage in upstate New York. The former owners of the house had tried to disguise its simple rural character by painting the exterior pearl gray and salmon pink. They had removed most of the small cottage windows and replaced them with jalousies—and putti statuary surrounded the turquoise swimming pool. The interior, with smoked-glass mirrors and vinyl floor tiles, was no more to my taste. But the land surrounding the house, with its stands of pine trees and ponds, was so beautiful and the price so low my husband convinced me I could transform it into our dream house. He asked me to close my eyes and imagine how perfect it would be when it was restored to its original rustic design. We bought the home, and we did just that. This is the master bedroom (left) of a home I had years later in the Hamptons on Long Island. It was an old horse barn that we converted into a living space. The final structure was simple and conformed to the original shape of the barn. The ceilings were vaulted, and some walls had wainscoting. The furnishings were minimal. My favorite piece in the master bedroom was this tester bed with its crocheted canopy. It reflected the airy, open atmosphere of the surrounding potato fields. When you stepped out on the balcony beyond the French doors you could survey the ever-changing landscape. It was always beautiful there: heavy fogs spread themselves over the fields and, on rare occasions, snow blanketed the flat land.

- The elements that make up an architectural style are numerous and varied. That's why it is important to consider each detail to determine which features are the most attractive and least attractive. No space is perfect, but by paying attention to the details you can make every space work decoratively.

- Plan your design around what you see when you look at the space as a whole. When the architecture connects the rooms, and you cannot be in one without seeing into the other, you must design the area as a whole.

- It's time to take an inventory of your home's architectural features, as they make up the anatomy of its rooms. To get you started, I have listed some of the most common architectural features on the following pages. Examine the examples in the photographs to see which are similar to what you have in your space. If your space has other architectural elements, write them down and photograph them if possible.

A while ago, my son Bill and his wife Elizabeth were in the middle of decorating their apartment in New York City. I remember a day when they were trying to decide whether to close off a second small doorway to the living room. They live in a very old apartment building—by New York standards at least—and one of its most attractive features was the handsome molding. The doorway in question was surrounded by this molding. However, it was not a necessary opening and took away needed wall space. One option was to close the opening and leave the molding as a frame for a wall mirror. Another option was to build shelves within the molding on the living room side. In the end, my son and his wife left the doorway alone, but this story just shows that there are often many solutions to architectural problems.

DOORS

PANELED DOOR

DOOR WITH DECORATIVE GLASS

FLUSH DOOR

SHOJI DOOR

FRENCH DOORS

SLIDING DOORS

Doors are decorative elements that are more important to the look of a home than you might think. If you don't have interesting doors, you can find them at local salvage companies that specialize in architectural artifacts. Don't overlook doors—they may open you up to new ideas.

STAINED-GLASS WINDOW

MULLIONS

SASH WINDOW

CASEMENT WINDOW

Never take windows for granted, even if their style is commonplace, because they are an integral part of your home's architecture. The division of glass and the way the windows operate influence your decoration. Windows are the most important source of light; the view from them can be enhanced or concealed. They are the eyes to outside.

SINGLE-GLASS CASEMENT WINDOW

TILT WINDOW

FLOORS

STONE

TILE AND STONE

WOOD PARQUET

WOOD HERRINGBONE

You can sense the material of a floor even before you see it. You know if it is slippery, soft, smooth, or bumpy. Add to this tactile sensation pattern and color and it becomes clear why the floor is another critical element of your decoration. If you don't like your floor, you can replace it, cover it, or color it. You need to relate your floor treatment to the decoration you are planning.

CERAMIC TILES

CARPET

WALLS

CERAMIC BRICK TILE

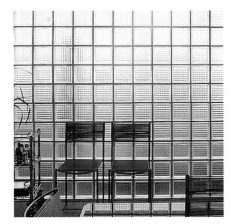

GLASS BRICK

STONE AND PLASTER

TILE

Walls are the largest surfaces of a room. They are the background for what stands or hangs in front of them. What are your walls made of? Are they all made of the same material or do they differ; plaster, brick, wood, sheetrock? Is a single wall divided into two materials—paneled below, plaster above, or tile and wood side by side? Does the material on the wall create a pattern, as with tile or paneling? Make note of all of the walls' characteristics—including the moldings.

WOOD PANELING

PAINTED PLASTER

CEILINGS

VAULTED CEILING

WOOD BEAMS

DECORATIVE PLASTER

DROPPED CEILING

The height of a ceiling is as important as the area of the floor. The two work in tandem and affect the feeling of the space. A ceiling's height changes optically depending on its material and color. Consider all the options available to you.

BARREL ARCH

FRESCOED CEILING

METHOD

3

TAKE INVENTORY

When you pass a shop window, you stop and look with interest at a new display. But if a shop window never changes, eventually you will walk by without looking in. When I had my shop, I made a point of changing the windows frequently, and I always sold the most out of the window on the day I changed the display.

It is difficult to stay interested in the things that surround us day after day. It is also extremely hard to be objective about what we possess, as there is always something that influences our point of view, be it a sentimental attachment to the object, its familiarity, its worth, or the time and cost required to replace it.

I have long admired the manner in which the traditional Japanese home honors the decorative object. There is, in these homes, an area called a *tokonoma*, or display alcove. Objects are carefully chosen and shown off here, and the display is changed on a seasonal basis. The thought is to reflect the seasons but also to refresh the eye regularly. This approach works for some painters, too: they turn their canvases to the wall for a period of time so that when they turn them back they see them anew. It is important to keep your eye fresh so you can evaluate what you own objectively.

There is no pleasant way to pack up all your belongings and move, but there are efficient ways to reduce confusion and speed things up. Use bright colored stickers to identify the contents of cartons, and make detailed lists of the contents on the box itself. Moving is also a time of decision and rediscovery: you may find something you had forgotten about or decide to dispose of what you don't like, don't use any more, or won't need in your new home.

• This procedure is more important for people who have already accumulated a household of furniture and objects, but it still applies to those starting out if they have been given or purchased anything. Evaluate every object and piece of furniture in your possession. Decide what you want to keep and what you need to eliminate.

• If you are moving to a new home, you should make your decisions to keep or eliminate an object based on the new environment. Sometimes an object that was wrong in one place can be made successful in another. Keep an open mind, but be careful not to keep anything you inherently dislike.

Imagine that your house is on fire. You only have enough time to grab your favorite things—what would you choose? Since this is not a real problem, don't base your decisions on intrinsic or sentimental value. Choose only what you like best. When you look at your possessions objectively, it clarifies how you feel about what you own. A successful interior design must be composed of objects you like, not diminished with objects you don't.

- Look back at your responses to Exercises 2, 3, 4, and 5 in Part I. When you did these exercises, you answered them instinctively because your choices weren't tied to your home and possessions. Now is the time to apply what you learned to your belongings, all those things you have purchased, inherited, or have been given—those things that are familiar, expensive, and sentimental. Don't underestimate the value of this exercise. One of the most difficult requirements in life is to step back and appraise a situation dispassionately. The question is: what works for you and what doesn't? It is much easier to get rid of a problem object in the beginning than to adjust your design to something you didn't like in the first place. You cannot make a strong design statement by incorporating elements you do not like: if you do, you weaken the concept.

- The painter Richard Diebenkorn said that still-life painting is "creating an intense unity from which everything dispensable has been removed." Of course, it might seem easier to accomplish this in a painting, which is not limited by practical considerations. Nevertheless, think of your room as an enormous still life. When you add an object that does not reinforce your design, you dilute what you are saying visually.

les mots qui ont un son noble
contiennent toujours de belles
images.
Marcel Pagnol

METHOD

4

FIND ECONOMICAL SOLUTIONS

The last time I moved, I decided to locate my painting studio at home, but I realized that doing so would make my buttermilk-colored, upholstered furniture impractical. So I went out and bought eighty yards of a very inexpensive, matte black, synthetic fabric that did not fray at the edges and draped easily. I was so anxious to get on with my work, I didn't even want to take the time to hem the fabric; I just tore it into lengths long enough to cover the upholstery completely. Within two hours my studio took on the look I wanted: simple black shapes contrasting with white walls. I was delighted with my inexpensive and easy solution. The fabric can be thrown into the washing machine whenever necessary. When we use the studio for entertaining, I throw pillows and quilts over the plain black material to make the space more interesting and decorative and bring in candles and flowers.

It's exciting to decorate from scratch, but most of us don't have the luxury. That's why it's important to be inventive and to familiarize yourself with methods to improve what you have. In many cases, furniture and objects that no longer please you can be transformed and work successfully again. There are four basic approaches to doing this: relocating, refinishing, re-covering, and camouflaging.

Decorating is always a challenge—and doing it within a budget is even harder. How do you revive a room's decoration economically? Here are a few ideas. One effective way is to group objects of the same material together and locate them in a place that will enhance them (opposite, top left). You can lend a simple decoration a poetic touch, as was done with this curtain (top right). You can artfully conceal shelves with an unattractive assortment of things with decorative doors (bottom left). Monogrammed tablecloths gathering dust in the closet can refresh an old sofa with new upholstery (bottom right).

RELOCATE OBJECTS AND FURNITURE

- Relocating is obviously the easiest and least expensive solution. Objects that are unsuitable in one location may be very successful in another. Experiment: try moving objects to different locations in the same room as well as to other rooms. Don't edit your thoughts or prejudge yourself—just try out the ideas that come to you. A crystal vase in a dark wood cabinet may look lifeless, but when relocated to a windowsill where the light can play on it, it sparkles.

This artful display of colored glass can be found in the home of the painter Robert Natkin. It's obvious that he had taken great care with the arrangement—considering carefully the spacing, size, and color of each object. His love of color is everywhere in his home: on many shelves he displays vividly glazed majolica; he has early American furniture in shades of ocher, iron red, and indigo; and his abstract paintings dance with color. He is a marvelous example of a person who responds to instinct, not intellect.

When you find a group of objects that capture your imagination experiment with them: try them in different locations, look at them from different vantage points, shuffle their arrangement, and combine them with fabrics, flowers, and fruit—anything you think will enhance the characteristic you want to emphasize.

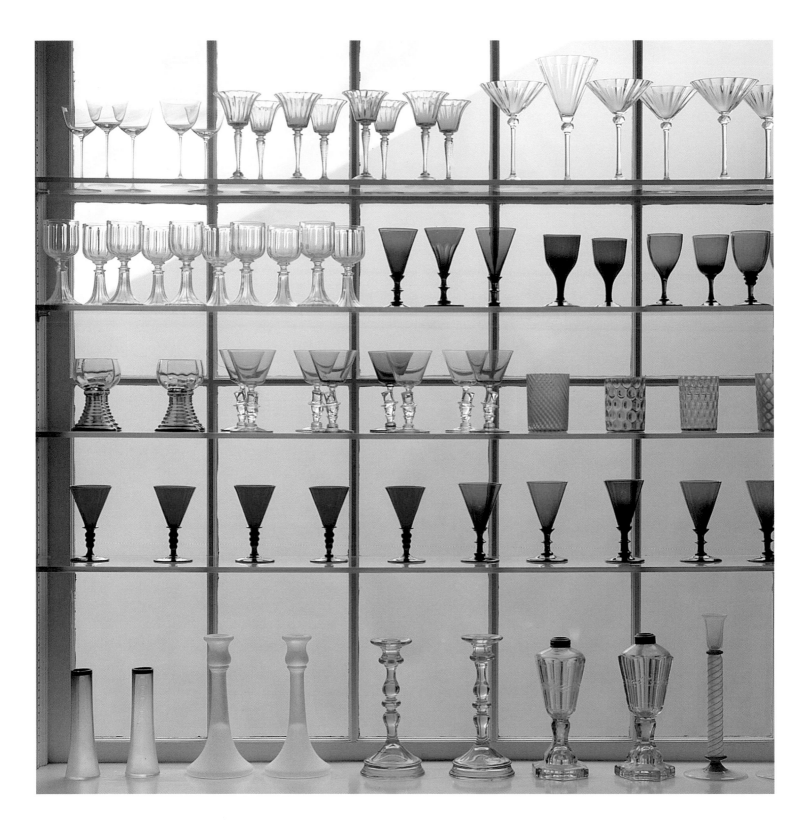

REFINISH FURNITURE

- There is more than one solution for altering the appearance of a piece of furniture. You can strip it, stain it, pickle it, polish or dull the surface, add a stencil, or paste on a decorative motif. Faux finishes are also effective—and there are hundreds of ways to create them. There are many books that provide step-by-step instruction on creating various finishes—they can also provide you with innovative ideas.

- When we were in the process of redoing our country house, we went with regularity to check the progress of the work. During one visit I encountered the painters stripping the old upstairs doors in preparation for painting. The doors had at least six layers of different paint colors. When I saw them in their partially stripped state the colors flickered on the surface and looked to me like the water in Monet's water lily paintings. I told the painter to stop and leave the doors just the way they were. He was a bit puzzled, but delighted to be relieved of the tedious job. These dappled doors are my favorite things in the house. Here is an example of refinishing which produced wonderful results.

This romantic building is a summer house in a picturesque New England village. From the windows, one can see the inspired gardens created by the owner. The whole house is an expression of his taste: it's evident in the antiques he buys and assembles, in the captivating freedom of his gardens which wend down the steep hillside to the river, and in the subtle paint finishes he uses to harmonize the antique architectural artifacts he builds into his rooms. He is a master of paint finishes; in this summer house he has stenciled the floor and refinished the walls to complement his acquisitions. He works with matte finishes and muted colors, and gives the surfaces a weathered appearance. Flowers from the garden are hung to dry and adorn the tranquil space with their faded color. Listen to your instinct and trust your ideas and imagination, just the way the owner of this little hideaway did. Choose the types of surfaces and paint effects you like, and explore how they can be used to improve your decoration.

METHOD

4

RE-COVERING

- This method uses flexible materials such as fabric, leather, and paper—anything you can glue, tack, nail, dye, paint, pleat, gather, bunch. In this way, you can re-cover a wall, box, window shade, counter, or shelf. Remember, reupholstering is only one way to re-cover something.

- Reupholstering may seem straightforward, but it can do more than re-cover: it can really transform the look of a sofa or chair in terms of its shape and style. I once reduced the bulkiness of a wing chair by having the upholsterer eliminate some of the padding on the frame. It's also possible to make side chairs more comfortable by adding padding to the seats or changing the style of a sofa by altering the number of cushions or by making a tight seat and back.

- You can also give a piece of furniture a new look by modifying certain details. By replacing synthetic stuffing with down, you can give pillows a more casual and expensive look. Changing the trimming or combining two different fabrics on the same piece is another approach. Discuss the different possibilities with the person who will do the work for you. Find out if the piece in question is worth the expense of reupholstering and, if so, what different modifications would improve its appearance.

The upholstery fabric on this low chair has been chosen thoughtfully, for it is the link that connects the elements of this simple decor. The square terra-cotta tiles on the floor and the rosy paint wash on the walls are echoed in the chair's unpretentious plaid covering. The chair's curved shape, a French style from the nineteenth century, has been updated with a geometric fabric, a practical covering for the country, because it does not show the wear and tear of outdoor living. This is why aesthetic and practical considerations go hand in hand when choosing upholstery fabric.

The manner in which a chair or sofa is covered is important, too, as it affects the chair's look. This chair has a tight seat and back and was covered in a plaid fabric; the result is neat and trim. It would have looked very different, for example, with a loose seat cushion, a dust ruffle, and floral fabric covering. Consider well the look that you want to give an upholstered piece, as reupholstering in the wrong style and fabric can be a costly mistake.

108

4

CAMOUFLAGE

- The purpose of camouflaging something is to make it blend in with its surroundings. If, for example, you have a large sofa whose shape no longer pleases you, you can diminish its presence in a room by covering it in a fabric that is the same color as the wall or rug. An old chair or sofa that's not worth reupholstering can be draped in a pretty fabric, too. For a long time, I had an exercise bike in the bedroom that was so ugly it detracted from everything else in the room. The bedroom is all white with a canopied bed and tables skirted with antique white linens. I draped a vintage sheet with a deep crocheted border over the bicycle and my eyesore vanished! By the same token, a functional object—such as a television or computer—that does not add to the decor of a room can be made more inconspicuous. In my country house, a bedroom that also serves as a television room is decorated with vintage Beacon blankets—I just drape one of them over the television when it is not in use.

There are numerous ways to transform those objects and pieces of furniture that no longer please you. Once you have clarified which objects need work, look through decorating magazines for specific examples of techniques you can use to improve what you have. There are also many wonderful books filled with ideas and step-by-step instructions for doing the work yourself, if you wish. When objects and furniture can not be improved, donate, sell, or give them away. This can be difficult to do and may seem extravagant, but in the long run it is more economical than compromising your taste. I have learned this lesson the hard way: more than once I have tried to force a piece of furniture or object to work in a design only to give up in frustration, annoyed at myself for having expended so much time and energy to arrive at the answer I instinctively knew from the start!

METHOD

5

PICK YOUR FOCUS

This room (opposite, top left) is organized around an unusual curved wall. This curve is accentuated by the long horizontal frame, the rounded built-in shelf and seat, and the semicircular table—all of which conform to the wall. The geometric motif of this mantle (top right) is echoed in the similar geometric motif in the rug. In this setting (bottom left), the grand piano, an impressive piece of furniture, dominates the space. The arrangement of furniture in this living room (bottom right) is organized around the painting over the sofa.

You have decided on your room's function, now you need to decide on its focus, that is, the feature around which you will build your decoration of the space. Choosing a focus is a question of establishing visual priorities, choosing the most interesting and significant decorative object. The possibilities are numerous: a painting, a sculpture, a tapestry, a screen, a canopy bed, a desk, a table, an armoire, a mirror, a chandelier, an architectural element such as a window or fireplace, or a color.

In one of my mother's homes, she subdivided a very long living room with two marbleized columns. They looked as if they were part of the original structure and made the space imposing—a quality my mother loved. But the room's focus was an impressive Art Nouveau majolica stove installed in the center of the main living room wall. The stove was the first thing you saw when you entered the room; its moss green and ocher glaze provided a color scheme for the space and its curved Art Nouveau shape was reflected in the line of the Venetian rococo furniture.

METHOD

The visual focus is the center of your design and everything else is built around it. Trust your instinct and choose a focal piece that you love.

- No matter whether your point of departure is an object or piece of furniture, measure it (if you can, photograph it) and determine where there is a prominent place to put it. If the piece goes on the wall, it should be visible immediately upon entering the space. If the room has more than one entryway, decide which is the principal entrance and provides the most dramatic view of the space. Then place the piece accordingly.

- An object suspended from the ceiling can be the focal point of a room. I once found a most unusual eighteenth-century chandelier that had blue and white Chinese porcelain pieces making up its core. The chandelier became the focus for the blue-and-white bedroom I had always wanted, thus simplifying my other decorating decisions. The drapery fabric I chose had a bold blue-and-white pattern, and I displayed all my blue-and-white delft platters and Chinese porcelain vases in the room, too. I also chose a large, blue oriental carpet with a subtle design, which provided a terrific background for the furniture and enhanced the blue in the chandelier.

The piano (opposite, top), with its imposing dark wood and voluptuous shape, commands attention in this pale, sparsely furnished space. The long dining table encircled by a set of elegant Arts & Crafts chairs (bottom) is the focus of this room. Note how the French doors, low ceiling, and simple light fixtures enhance the focal point and further emphasize its importance in the setting. To define a visual center and organize a decor, it is helpful to keep in mind the decorations you have seen in the past which captured your imagination. My visit to Boscobel, a historic house on the Hudson River, had a lasting impression upon me. The interior walls were freshly painted a luminous yellow color. I was so taken with the color, I painted the walls in my living room the same yellow. That said, traveling is a wonderful way to gain inspiration. Photographing what inspires you gives you a permanent reminder and helps you put the ideas into play in your home.

The interior of this houseboat (opposite, top) is casual and intriguing. It is decorated around the long horizontal window, which frames the outside world as if it were a painting. Unusual shapes in unexpected locations can be exciting in design because they add an element of surprise. This loft space (bottom) has been divided by two majestic wooden columns, and their color merges with the cinnabar red of the walls. Like two enormous tree trunks growing through the ceiling, they lend an air of dignity to the interior. Note how the other furnishings are small in scale and keep the eye's focus on the columns.

- If the room you're decorating has an interesting architectural element, think about arranging the room to show it off. If you'd like the focus to be architectural, but have nothing of architectural interest in your space, you can introduce one. Today, there are many stores that specialize in selling original and reproduction decorative architectural elements such as mantles, paneling, corner cupboards, and wood-burning stoves. These are my favorite type of stores, and I always search them for an interesting architectural point of departure when I am about to start a decoration. Doing so is an easy way for me to find a focus.

- You can also transform or eliminate existing architectural elements. When my husband and I bought a small farmhouse, we gutted all the walls and replaced the windows and doors. The house had been altered so many times over the years with poorly constructed additions that its original eighteenth-century structure was hidden. We wanted to restore its original look, so after everything was dismantled, we reconstructed the house with architectural artifacts found locally and in keeping with the original construction.

COLOR

METHOD

- If you have a passion for a particular color or want to use a color as the focal point of a room, that color determines your background: the walls, ceiling, woodwork, and floors. You have to decide how you want to use it: as a paint, fabric, wallpaper, or a combination of these. In Exercises 6 and 7 in Part I (see pages 54–80), you learned how to describe color better, to understand some of the technical characteristics of color, and to define which color concepts you prefer. If you choose to make color your focus, keep the results of those exercises in mind. The color you use will affect everything in view and radically alter the room; it is the catalyst for all other choices and must be your first consideration.

- To choose the right color for your purposes, go to a paint store and select at least seven samples in the color family you are considering. Remember that a tiny swatch of color is not going to reveal the effect the color is going to have in your space. All colors look darker and brighter covering a large area than they do on a swatch. A cost-effective and timesaving procedure is to first buy the smallest possible amount of the color and paint samples on the walls of your room.

    To test the color, make large samples, about two feet by two feet. Begin at the edge of the wall, not in the middle. Paint your sample on a wall that receives sunlight and on one that doesn't. It is also helpful to paint a large sample in a corner where the walls intersect.

    If you think you like the color, live with it for a couple of days to see it at different times of day. Observe how the color looks with the furniture and objects you are planning to use in the space. Most importantly, ask yourself if you like the color enough to live with it all the time. By following these steps you will be able to judge more easily and accurately whether the color you have chosen works long term in the area you are decorating.

Here is an example of a room in which the decoration is organized around a color. Blue is a tranquil color and this parlor is very peaceful. The owners of this house love to escape to the country to garden, read, and write. The gardens surrounding the house have a feeling of uninhibited abandon and abound with splashes of vivid color. If Jackson Pollock had been a gardener, not a painter, I think his gardens would have looked like these. The purple irises in the vase complement the color scheme.

METHOD

6

MAKE A FURNITURE PLAN

There are two ways to create a balance in decorating: symmetry and asymmetry. A symmetrical arrangement, as shown in this library (opposite, top right) and exemplified by the vase placed in the middle of a bureau (bottom left), is easier to understand, because objects are either centered or arranged so every object placed on one side is balanced by an object of equal visual weight on the other. This is particularly simple when arranging pairs of objects, but objects similar in size, shape, and color can be used as well. When the balance is determined by an asymmetrical placement (top left), the objects are often different sizes and shapes. Here, the cushions and blue built-in shelf are balanced by the dark fretted doorway on the far wall. The dining room (bottom right) is another example of asymmetrical balance.

The blue area of the room, because of its darker color, balances the light section that is furnished with a table and chairs. The blue ceiling bridges the two areas.

When I was a little girl, I didn't have a doll's house, but I did have some shelves in my closet that were mine to use as I wished. I would arrange all the small things I collected on them. I changed the arrangements often, and because the objects were small, making changes was very easy.

Imagine how much less intimidating decorating would be if you could decorate your room in miniature and then enlarge it to its actual size. Sometimes the scale of the room and furniture can be overwhelming, which is why decorators, set designers, and architects use scale models. Models help them understand the space and permit them to experiment with countless ideas before committing to the final design.

Simple models are not difficult to build out of cardboard. You do not have to indicate every little twist and turn; make your forms very basic. What is most important is to make everything conform to the same scale; in this way you can place your models on the floor plan and try out different arrangements.

Arranging furniture is an act of creating a visual equilibrium. This visual balance has nothing to do with an object's physical weight, but with its visual weight. Achieving a visual equilibrium that is pleasing to you is the result of the way you place furniture and objects in a room. To keep a row boat in balance, for example, the occupants are arranged according to their size, weight, and function (who's going to row). Similarly, a room is in balance when the furniture is arranged according to its size, visual weight, and function.

METHOD

- A room is a box with three large surfaces: the floor, the walls, and the ceiling. Start this procedure by making an exact floor plan of the room. If you already have a floor plan, you'll save time, but make sure it is to scale.

- There are no rules for creating a balanced room—only concepts to keep in mind. In order to arrange furniture in the most logical way, arrange the objects on the floor before putting objects on the walls or hanging them from the ceiling. The only exception to this rule is if your focus is on a wall or ceiling. In those circumstances, the focus will influence the floor arrangement. The most obvious example of the focus being on the wall is a fireplace, which determines the placement of all the furniture in the room. An important chandelier is an example of a ceiling object determining your furniture arrangement, as is sometimes the case in a formal dining room.

This contemporary room is a good example of a thoughtfully conceived floor plan. The black-and-white color scheme makes the placement of furniture and objects very visible. The two low sofas against the wall fit perfectly in the corner of the room and under the window. The cantilevered black table juts out from the opposite wall and reaches toward the black sofas to create an asymmetrical balance. The table has been built for the space and provides a functional as well as aesthetic purpose. It repeats the horizontal line of the sofas and the low flat ceiling. Vertical and organic, the two large plants interrupt the room's horizontal emphasis and provide visual relief from the sleek black surfaces.

METHOD

- Take some newspaper and lay it out on the floor so that it corresponds in size to the furniture you intend to use. The more accurate your newspaper shapes are, the easier it is to understand the dimensions of your furniture and place it. You may wish to label the pieces of newspaper and try them in other rooms, making this method an easy way to experiment with different furniture arrangements. Making a furniture plan—determining the amount of space the furniture will occupy and its location—is the first of three critical steps to achieving balance in a room. The other two—height and mass—are discussed on pages 127–130. Keep in mind the traffic pattern in the room, too; a busy doorway should not be impeded by anything that interferes with the flow of activity.

- If you are considering a patterned floor—be it tile, stone, marquetry, or stenciled—take the time to lay out the pattern with pieces of the actual material, if you can. Otherwise, do a mock-up using sheets of paper that match the colors you are considering and arrange them in the intended pattern. You can affix the pieces of paper to each other with transparent tape.

This dining room is organized around three large objects: a painting, a dining table, and a breakfront. They are of a similar color and visual weight, and the checkerboard floor pattern connects them. The chairs and standing lamp are slim and do not have much visual impact. Floors with dark and light alternating squares command attention. I have loved them since I studied the Flemish painters of the seventeenth century, who often depicted interiors with checkerboard floors. This was the pattern of the floor in the entrance hall, living room, and dining room of my first apartment.

METHOD

7

CREATE A VISUAL BALANCE

The four pictures on the opposite page are examples of elevation, the way in which an object on the floor intersects with the wall, windows, and other architectural features in the room. This bulky but airy and lightweight-looking bird cage (top left) is placed between French doors (not seen) and the windows of this garden room to lend a sense of mass without weight. This grandfather clock (top right) stands in front of a paneled dado and next to a doorway. The pictures hanging to its right are positioned to relate to its height. These floor-to-ceiling bookcases (bottom left) draw attention to the room's high ceiling. This stocky file cabinet (bottom right) reaches the height of the middle of the window, while the vase of hydrangeas on top is at about the same level as the top of the window.

Remember your class picture at school—how the teacher would arrange all the students according to height, with the taller pupils in the back and the shorter ones up front? The same approach is relevant to decorating because it is essential to be conscious of how objects and furniture relate to each other in terms of height. Knowing the height of a piece of furniture and how it relates to other pieces in the room as well as windows, doorways, and other structural wall elements is essential. When one piece of furniture is free-standing but next to another, the heights of both pieces must work together. The same thing is true when a piece is placed along a wall, next to a window, or near a doorway. The relationship between the height of the furnishings in your room to its architecture is referred to as visual balance, and it is critical to creating a successful decoration.

METHOD

- The floor plan and the newspaper that you used in Method 6 (see page 124) are two-dimensional and do not inform you about the height of the furniture in relationship to the walls. You are now going to make an elevation plan for your room, that is, a diagram of the vertical surfaces. A floor plan and an elevation plan are an integral part of every professional designer's work. The elevation plan should indicate the location and size of all openings, recesses, and protrusions, such as doors, windows, niches, fireplaces, built-ins, columns, radiators, vents, and so forth. Use your floor plan to make the elevation plan. Make a number of photocopies of the floor and elevation plan, and always keep a set with you. Nothing is more frustrating than seeing something you like—be it in a local store or a shop abroad—and not being able to make a decision about buying it because you don't know if the dimensions are right, or even worse, buying the piece and finding it doesn't fit.

- You will need a yardstick to compare the height of the piece of furniture with something stationary on the wall. Measure to see whether your furniture is the same height as the top, middle, or bottom edge of the window, and how it relates in height to the doorways. If the piece is against the wall, put tape with low adhesion (most masking tape works for this purpose) on the wall to mark its height. Be aware that if you place a large, tall object near the entrance of a room doing so will create an emotional barrier at the entrance. High-standing furniture can be intimidating when encountered upon first entering a room, whereas when placed further from the room's entrance, the piece can be seen in its entirety and the space stays open and inviting.

Every room offers many different decorating possibilities. The furniture in this room has been kept low. The chaise lounge and sofa leave a large area of bare white wall exposed, and the dark beamed ceiling creates a frame for the eye. Except for the wooden shutters, all the vertical furnishings are white and blend into the wall, another way of emphasizing the horizontal plane. The light fixtures are functional, and the shapes of the furniture, strong. The only patterned object is the oriental area rug in the foreground, which picks up the blue color of the sofa. The asymmetrical placement of the picture over the sofa balances the back of the chaise lounge in the foreground.

7

- The solidity and visual weight of an object are very important considerations when arranging furniture. A cabinet made of rattan and another in oak can have identical dimensions but a very different visual weight. The oak appears massive, while the rattan appears lighter and easier to move; this difference creates an emotional reaction. In addition to its dimensions, the mass of an object is another critical element in creating visual equilibrium. Sometimes you need an object that feels sturdy and solid, and sometimes an object that is large but lightweight is better. The use of large floor plants or a decorative folding screen is a way to introduce something with height and volume that is not massive. Objects that are tall but not weighty are often the perfect solutions to balancing a room's arrangement.

- Part of your work as a designer is to consider in your design the visual weight of an object as well as its actual weight. Glass tables look light even though glass is heavy. A wood armoire looks heavy—and it is. A round marble tabletop on a slender pedestal base does not look massive, although it probably weighs a great deal. The sensation of lightness or heaviness and the size of an object make up the points that need to be taken into account when you place furnishings in a room. That said, it's still important to place instinct before logic. Design always gets back to the way something makes you feel: trust your sense of design and balance the room the way it feels most comfortable to you, but you must judge the room or area as a whole.

The first time I saw a *tansu* staircase, I was visiting a friend in Kyoto, a master of the tea ceremony, who had a tea house in his garden. After that visit I searched every antique store I passed until I found and bought one—not exactly a small purchase you can tuck in your suitcase! What I love most is the powerful shape and simple construction of these staircases, which one finds in traditional Japanese country homes. In their original locations, the staircases provided access to an upper floor. The interior of a *tansu* is enormous, making it an excellent place to conceal unattractive electronic equipment. In this case, I used the steps to display my Japanese basket collection and store papers. Sadly, when I moved, I had to part with it: I knew it would never suit my new space.

METHOD

8

SUBDIVIDE THE WALLS

When subdividing the space on a wall, don't hesitate to use multiple shapes, colors, and materials. The arrangement of these etchings (opposite, top left) is regimented and symmetrical, while the arrangement composed of a mirror and several paintings (top right) is balanced asymmetrically. The small keepsakes enclosed in the white rectangular molding (bottom left) create a composition of round and square shapes. These decorative storage shelves (bottom right) have staggered vertical and horizontal supports that create interesting cubicles for displaying objects.

I remember the first time I participated in hanging pictures on a wall. I was about six years old, and my family had moved into a spacious apartment on Central Park in New York City. The walls of my bedroom were pale peony pink, my favorite color at the time. One day my mother brought home a set of pictures of birds. There were twelve in all, all the same size, and framed in an unusual blue velvet. She asked me to hold up a picture against the pink wall and called in my brother to hold up some, too. When she seemed to know how she wanted to proceed she enlisted my father's help to put nails in the wall at the measured intervals that pleased her. I remember thinking "I never saw anyone hang pictures one above another before. I don't like it," but my opinion was not asked at the time. Nonetheless, I grew proud of my birds perched on the wall.

Your wall is a canvas, so examine its shape—whether it is vertical or horizontal in emphasis—as this will affect the number, placement, and size of the pictures or objects you hang on it. Once you have an idea of what you want to hang on the wall, you have to decide on the spacing between the pictures or objects. This is what painters call negative space and it is just as important to the success of your composition as the objects themselves. Pictures placed too close together may look congested and not in balance with the remaining negative space or bare wall; by the same token, things placed too far apart may look fragmented and unrelated. When you hang objects or pictures, you are creating a visual rhythm, and the eye moves to the beat of your arrangement. The rhythm you establish should suit the mood you want to create.

METHOD

- When you hang pictures on a wall you are literally subdividing that surface to compose an arrangement you find pleasing. There are no rules about how pictures or any other objects should subdivide a wall, as this is a subjective decision. Nonetheless, be aware of the effect you are creating. Painters, for example, check their work all the time by stepping back from it in order to see how what they have done affects the work as a whole.

- Imagine a group of eleven pictures of different sizes, shapes, and subjects—the combinations are endless. Play with different arrangements, trying all the combinations you can think of before you make a final decision. Design, above all, is about exploration. Since you can't hang the pictures without making marks on the wall, lean them up against the wall first; galleries do this before an exhibition because it allows them to arrange and rearrange the art before hanging it. You could also make some rough diagrams on paper to explore other layouts or place the pictures flat on the floor so you can have more than one row. Having someone hold them up for you can be helpful, too. Use the method that works for you.

These pictures are the work of artist Alan McCollum and are a play on the shape of a rectangle. The variation occurs not in the depiction of different images within the frame but in the subtle difference in the color of the frames, the size and shape of the black area in the center of each frame, and the way they relate to each other on the wall. The pictures work as a unit, and the straight line of the black sofa gives the frames a base. The result is a bold graphic composition. The elimination of all color, except for tones of gray, is a daring statement and makes you rethink and expand all your preconceived ideas about pictures.

8

- Many things can subdivide a wall other than pictures and paintings: a tapestry, a mirror, a mural, a bas-relief, sconces, fabric hangings, shelves, and vitrines are all possibilities. As you subdivide a wall, you must continue to take into account the elevation of the room and the location of the furniture. In most cases, the arrangement of furniture determines where you locate objects on the wall. Of course, there are exceptions, most notably when the object on the wall is the focal point of the room: then the furniture is arranged in relationship to it.

- There is hardly a home that does not have shelves. Most people don't think of them as subdividing a wall, but they do. Whether you build them in or add one or more to a finished wall, their placement is very important. First, you need to consider the distance between the shelves, whether it will be uniform, graduated, or at some other interval. You'll need to determine whether the shelves will be stationary or adjustable, and whether you want them to blend in with the color of the wall or to stand out decoratively. Of course, you also need to consider what are you going to put on the shelves, too, be they objects, pictures, books, or a combination of things.

In this kitchen, the shelves are painted the same color as the walls. What calls attention to their arrangement and the way the shelves have subdivided the wall are the objects on them. What an imaginative decoration for a kitchen—a collection of lids in procession: they differ in size and shape, but are similar in texture and color. The rack running above the counter holds an assortment of utensils unified by color and silhouette. This photograph demonstrates how the form of an object can be used to make a strong visual statement.

METHOD

9

ARRANGE STILL LIFES

Here are four types of decorative still lifes. The table setting (opposite, top left) is a composition of matte, shiny, and woven textures, and round and rectangular shapes in shades of rust and gray. In this still life (top right), the burled wood tabletop creates a warm, lustrous background for a collection of wonderful smooth, rounded objects. The large stone placed between the table legs balances the whole composition and echoes the shapes above. These metal vases, bowls, and candlesticks stretch across my mantle shelf (bottom left) in single file, accentuating its length—their strong silhouettes merge with the delicate floral motifs in silver overlay. These statuesque oriental porcelains staggered in height and placement are combined with the airy grace of a Japanese lantern (bottom right).

Still-life arrangements demand the same considerations as arranging furniture, but on a smaller scale. Every composition, large or small, deals with the symmetrical or asymmetrical placement of objects; each object's size, bulk, and height; each object's form, color, pattern, and texture; and the negative space between the objects. This is not a complicated and cerebral process but an instinctive one that calls upon creative awareness and imagination to achieve the best results.

Artists Chardin, Cézanne, Braque, and Morandi were known for their still-life paintings. They loved painting simple objects because they were fascinated by how objects arranged on a surface related to each other in terms of color, shape, size, and texture. When they created these still-life compositions, they were also subdividing, or segmenting, the surface on which they placed the objects.

Segmenting is something you do all the time without thinking. Every time you place an object on a surface you are segmenting that surface. When you set a table, the dishes, cutlery, linens, and glasses segment the surface of the table. Now that you know how to arrange your furniture (see Method 7, pages 126–131), you can move on to placing objects on the furniture and other horizontal surfaces of your room to create a still life.

- A still life can consist of a single object or fifty. It can be composed of any combination of small objects: boxes, plates, vases, framed pictures, arrangements of flowers, fruit, lamps, stones, shells, sculptures, pillows, collectibles, quilts, and so on. A still life need not be restricted to a table top. Any horizontal surface can serve as your canvas.

- When you want to create a still life, begin with its location. The size of the surface, the material of which it is made, and its background will determine your selections. Don't create a still life and then try to find a place for it—this would be like choosing accessories before you know what you are going to wear. When you create a still life, look at the entire setting—the nature of the surface and what is behind that surface (window, wall, open space), the color and material of the wall (paint, fabric, mirror), and the source of light. When you select a still-life location, you must also determine the viewpoint from which it will be seen. Is the viewpoint at eye level, below eye level or above eye level? Of course, one's eye level changes just by sitting down, so decide which viewpoint is the most important to you and shows off the objects to their best advantage. I am always reminded of the importance of viewpoint when I go to the theater. When I sit in the mezzanine I am often surprised at how much attention the set designer has given to the floor of the stage, sometimes it's painted to look like tile, marble, or an oriental rug. The spectators in the orchestra have no idea the floor has been decorated because they can't see it.

Here, the jagged edge of this staircase is in opposition to the bulbous shape of the four storage jars. The drop-leaf table with its outstretched, winglike supports balances the voluminous black shapes on top. This still life defies conventional arrangements because it places a group of objects that appear too weighty for the slender support of the table beneath. Yet it is this very contradiction that catches the eye.

• Look around the room you are decorating and choose a place (or places) you want to enhance with a grouping of objects. Then select the best objects for that location; chances are, you will need to try many different objects to find what works best. A tall vase placed below eye level will appear shorter, perhaps too short, while a shallow bowl placed above eye level will be difficult to see. Museum curators are always mindful to display an object to its best advantage, and that is your job too when creating a still life. If you have selected a mantle shelf or a coffee table, look at the objects you have placed there from the perspective of sitting and standing. Be conscious of objects that obstruct a conversation area: a large flower arrangement on a dining table might be appealing when the table is not in use, but it may be in the way when people are seated. That's why it's important to be equally aware of the practical and the aesthetic when placing objects.

In the entrance foyer of our apartment I had a carpenter install a shelf to encircle the space. The shelf runs continuously and is lined up with the top of the doors, well above eye level. I can see into the foyer when I am painting and did not want to have any object at eye level to distract me. However, I did want the foyer to be interesting to someone entering the apartment. The shelf is painted the same linen white as the walls and displays my collection of ikebana baskets. These baskets are among my favorite things, and I wanted to show them off to their best advantage. Now when entering the apartment, the first thing that is seen are these extraordinary baskets with their unusual shapes, imaginative weaves, and dark, aged, bamboo patina silhouetted against the light walls.

METHOD

10

ILLUMINATE THE SPACE

Lighting fixtures should not be an afterthought, but part of the decorating scheme. This wall light (opposite, top left) throws the light up, bouncing it off the ceiling and wall, and so illuminates the space indirectly, while the floor lamp (top right) casts the light down. The mirrored sconce with its undulating frame (bottom left) captures the flickering light of candles and adds a festive air. This utilitarian professional light is a streamlined addition to a turn-of-the-century space; its large, concave reflector beams the light upward.

I once read about a celebrated Hollywood movie star in the forties who was advised by her decorator not too worry about the harsh light in her makeup area because if she could make herself look good under those conditions she would look fabulous everywhere else. I don't agree. When you are choosing lighting for your home you want to control the effect.

When posing for a photograph, I would rather be well lit then made up by the world's most talented makeup artist. Light is transforming. A theater set is lifeless until the lighting engineer works his magic, creating an air of mystery or the mundane, establishing day or night, evoking a sense of heaven or hell. The director and lighting engineer work hand in hand to tell the story. Your house is your set design, and you are the director and lighting engineer in one. You must light your space to tell your story.

Another consideration when illuminating a space is natural light. If sunlight streams through the space at certain times of day, you will need to consider, if necessary, appropriate window treatments to control the amount of light entering the room. Areas with the potential to be gloomy can be helped by installing frosted glass. In our country house all of the doors off the center hall have frosted glass filling the upper panel; even when the doors to the rooms off the hallway are closed, the sunlight from these spaces keeps the hall illuminated and inviting. Frosted glass is readily available at any glass and mirror supplier, comes in a variety of textures, and is not expensive. Bathroom doors often offer perfect conditions for frosted glass panels, since light can be spread from one space to the next and privacy maintained.

METHOD

- Today, the choice of lighting fixtures available is vast—from the simple, warm, and inviting candle to high-tech, ceiling-installed spotlights. The look, function, and atmosphere you wish to create determine the lighting fixtures you choose: they are the criteria that guide you. Lighting can be used to highlight or diminish, dramatize or neutralize objects in a room. With the turn of a rheostat, your room can be transformed from dark and mysterious to bright and friendly. That is why it is so important to decide where you want to locate your lighting fixtures as well as what kind and quality of light you are after. Do you want ambient light, spotlights, incandescent or fluorescent light—or some combination of these?

- Begin by deciding the placement of the lights in a room as well as the quality of the light you want there. If you choose to install spotlights on the ceiling or lights on the wall, or have lighting fixtures that require additional outlets, plan for these before making your alterations. It is much easier, neater, and safer to prepare properly for additional wiring and outlets in advance than to jury-rig extension cords later.

The recessed lights in the ceiling of this room were built in during its construction. The lights flood the wall and the distance between each fixture creates arcs of light on the wall above the painting. When you position ceiling lights, be they recessed or track, you need to consider the following factors: the distance between the fixture and the wall, the space between each fixture, and the area you want to illuminate. If you have inherited recessed fixtures from a previous tenant, adjustments are possible. The spread of the light can be altered by changing the bulb. Sometimes a louver can be fitted over the "can" to change the direction of the light. Track lighting is economical and is often the only choice if you have old ceilings. The tracks are attached to the ceiling and accommodate a variety of fixtures.

Today's technology provides a wealth of lighting solutions. There are three basic types of lightbulbs: incandescent, fluorescent, and halogen. The first gives off a light that is warmer because it is more yellow. Fluorescent light is cooler and bluer—more like daylight. That said, enormous progress has been made in this area, and you can find incandescent bulbs that give off light that approximates daylight and fluorescent bulbs with an incandescent glow. Halogen bulbs produce an intense light, which can be desirable for desk work, reading, or highlighting an art object. Lights that use this type of bulb come in a wide variety of styles.

Once you know what effect you want to create, find out what's available. Be specific. Do you want a lighting fixture that is decorative or simply functional and unobtrusive? Do you want dramatic lighting or evenly distributed, general illumination? Will you be changing the mood of the room from one function to another, such as from work to entertaining? (If your answer is yes, you will need a good direct light for working and indirect, warm, atmospheric light for receiving guests.) Are you planning to electrify an old fixture or make a lamp from an object such as a vase? Do you want floor lamps or table lamps or both? The combinations are endless. If you are not sure about what you want, go back and look through magazines to find examples of lighting concepts and fixtures that were in rooms you liked.

If you want lamps with lamp shades, then you will have to consider the shades' shape, size, and material. When you go to buy a lamp shade, always bring your lamp and the dimensions of the space where it will be placed. This is a nuisance, but it will save you time in the long run because you will be able to experiment with different lamp shades as well as consider them in relationship to the lamp base and the lamp's location.

This bedroom has two types of lighting. The small wall lights provide general illumination, while the lamps with opaque shades, light for reading. Having different sources of light is important because it allows you to tailor the lighting for the occasion.

METHOD

11

WORK WITH MIRRORS

Mirrors are magical. The splendor of the Hall of Mirrors at Versailles is a breathtaking sight. Imagine how spectacular it must have been for a visitor in the eighteenth century when it was lit by candles and filled with lavishly dressed courtiers reflected ad infinitum. The most august ambassador was surely dazzled. What better entrance hall for Louis XIV, the Sun King?

Mirrors have long held a place in decoration and in art. The Flemish masters loved to reflect an entire room in a convex mirror, and Manet's painting *Bar at the Folies-Bergère* draws the viewer into the painting by reflecting the exciting night-life of Paris in a large mirror.

Mirrors are powerful decorating tools. They can make the smallest area seem spacious; they can be functional or decorative, confuse and distort. Learn how to use them to your advantage.

Mirrors are a great way to create the illusion of space, but they must be well situated or you may end up reflecting something you wish to de-emphasize. When I was twelve, I went on my first apartment-looking expedition with my mother. The apartment we looked at had been owned by an elderly woman who had not attended to the place for a long time. My mother was good at seeing beyond surface conditions, so the dingy walls,

"Mirror, mirror, on the wall, who's the fairest of them all?" The Queen in Snow White knew the power of mirrors. With a mirror, you can visually double the size of a room, as is the case here (opposite, top left). You can also create a sense of expansiveness when you install a mirror from floor to ceiling, as was done in this foyer (top right). A mirror can also offer another view of the architecture in an impressive space as well as provide a convenient place to check your appearance when you enter or leave (bottom left). You can rest a mirror against the wall (bottom right) to get a full view of yourself when you are dressing. A large portable mirror is a good way to experiment—move it to different locations and see where it most enhances the space.

broken lights, stained carpeting, and musty draperies did not discourage her. I remember her commenting on a floor-to-ceiling mirror at the end of a dark hallway. She said it exaggerated the length and darkness of the hall and if she took the apartment it would be the first thing she'd remove—which is exactly what she did.

When I moved into my present apartment, I removed everything the former owner had installed except for some built-in bookcases and a wall of mirrors in the room next to my studio. There is a very large opening between my studio and this other room, and the mirror, which is in front of you upon entering, makes the rooms appear much larger. This mirrored wall is very convenient when I am working, because I can check my paintings in the mirror as I go. The mirror provides a fresh perspective of the work by increasing the distance between me and the painting. When we entertain, the area is easily transformed for guests. Candles shimmer and bouquets of flowers look even more glamorous reflected in the mirrored wall.

Because this mirror is hung horizontally, it provides a wide view of the space. The tomato-red walls envelop the visitor, and the bright outdoors is absorbed by their rich color. The earthenware vessels, some enormous, are another dramatic gesture. The beautiful Italian velvet draped over one corner of the long table provides an interesting contrast to the coarse clay.

- The function of a mirror is to reflect. Therefore, when its function is to reflect accurately what is in front of it, it must located and lit with care. When installing mirrors in bathrooms, closets, and dressing rooms, make sure the mirror provides a flawless reflection and that the light is becoming, not harsh. But when you want a mirror to add a sense of space—and when positioned properly, a mirror can make a room seem twice its size—the criteria is different.

- Before you install a mirror in a room, be sure you will like what it reflects. Experiment with it in different locations before hanging it. If you have a large portable mirror, bring it to the location you are considering. Even though the portable mirror may not be the same size and style as the mirror you plan to install, it will give you an idea of what the reflection will be.

- Framed mirrors are decorative as well as useful. Because they are easy to move, it is possible to try them in different locations without much effort. There are probably as many types of framed mirrors as light fixtures, so explore what's available. Again, re-examine your YES choices for mirror affects you like as well as look through books and magazines for mirrors installed in interesting ways.

CONCLUSION

The most exciting thing about creativity is the way it unfolds constantly. If you look at the work of any great artist, you will see evolution. At the Tate Gallery in London, I once saw a retrospective of painter Mark Rothko. Rothko's early work was representational, and at first I thought it seemed unrelated to his later abstract canvases. But the more I studied the early paintings, the more apparent his unique aesthetic—which had always been evolving—became for me.

Your aesthetic is your signature—it is yours and yours alone. Nourish it and it will become strong, distinctive, and continue to evolve.

ENJOY CREATING YOUR DECORATING STYLE.

WORKBOOK

QUESTIONNAIRE

Can you define what you have learned about your taste and style? Are you now able to identify and describe precisely the feelings which were so illusive before? The more specific you can be about your taste, the better you can express it. When you feel you are asserting your ideas in decorating, you have become a designer.

Tests and questionnaires can help us learn more about ourselves. In the following questionnaire, you are going to evaluate and outline your taste in order to determine what you have learned about your decorating style.

1] What have you discovered about your taste that you didn't know before?

_____
_____
_____

2] Does your decoration reflect the rooms and objects you liked in the exercises in Part I?

_____
_____
_____

3] Are there any instances where you have compromised your taste? Are you resorting to old habits when you didn't have an immediate design solution?

_____
_____
_____

4] Does your completed "jigsaw puzzle" create a picture you like?

_____
_____
_____

5] Are you pleasantly surprised and pleased with the way you decorate?

_____

_____

_____

6] Do you feel your style and taste reflect who you are?

_____

_____

_____

7] How would you describe your style? Circle all answers that apply and add other descriptions, if necessary.

restrained	flamboyant
serious	playful
minimalist	traditional
colorful	plain
ornate	informal
formal	sophisticated
relaxed	urbane
rustic	

8] How would you describe your personality? Circle all answers that apply and add other descriptions, if necessary.

quiet	cautious
talkative	impulsive
shy	extroverted
cheerful	home-oriented
friendly	changeable
opinionated	consistent
confident	unpredictable
thoughtful	predictable
subdued	acquisitive
adventurous	modest
daring	

9] What have you discovered when you decorate your way? Are you comfortable or uncomfortable with the following decorating conditions and environments? Check all that apply in the corresponding column.

	COMFORTABLE	UNCOMFORTABLE
decorating changes		
clutter		
sleek		
old-fashioned		
avant-garde		
exotic		
homey		
empty		
dark		
luminous		
spacious		
quaint		
bright colors		
pastel colors		
colorless		
contrasting		
crowded		
dainty		
massive		
romantic		
formal		
traditional		

10] Do you see a connection between your personality and the way in which you decorate?

_____

_____

_____

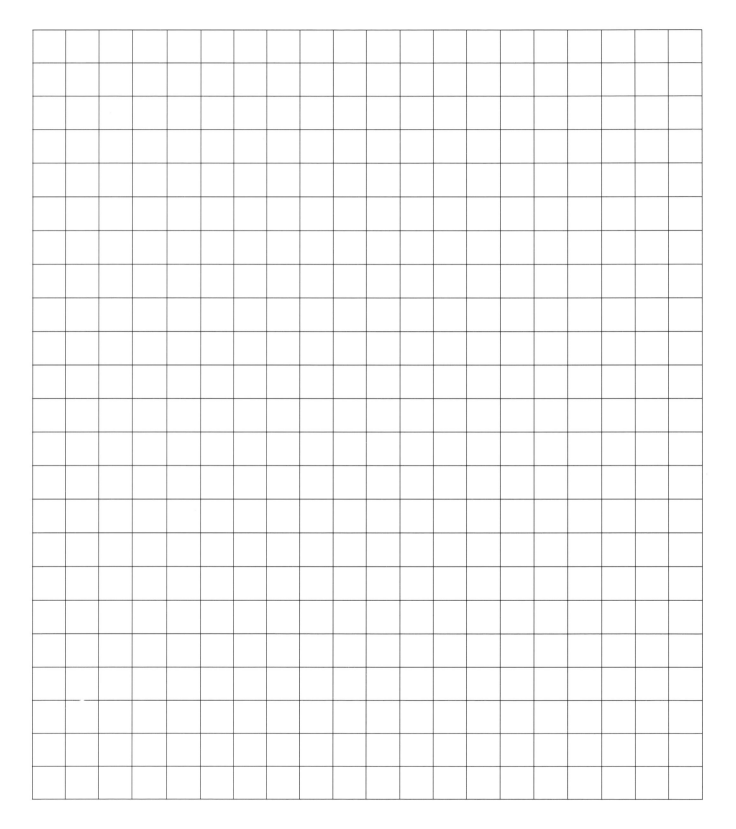

NOTES

NOTES

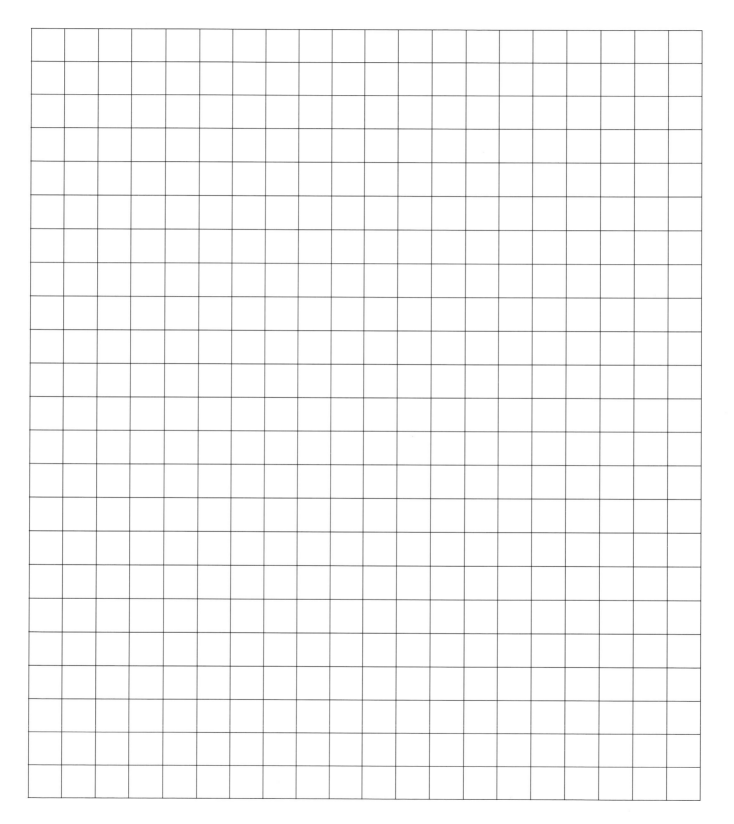

ACKNOWLEDGMENTS

Many people encouraged me during the creation and process of publishing this book, and I would like to thank them for their enthusiasm, candid reactions, and insightful suggestions. First, I'd like to thank June Weir, who encouraged me to write a book about my ideas, and my brother Andrew Stewart, who believed in the uniqueness of the concept from the start and offered his expert publishing advice so freely. I am also grateful to Susie Townsend and Christine Kinser, who were full of creative suggestions, to my daughter Victoria Love and my daughter-in-law Elizabeth Love, who asked many helpful and practical questions, and to my son Bill Love, whose technical wizardry saved me from many a computer meltdown. But above all, I would like to thank my husband Bob Frye, whose countless hours of reading and commenting on revisions as I typed them provided the steadying hand that kept me going. I was only able to take the many photographs in this book because of the access my friends gave me to their homes; for their kindness in this regard I would like to thank: Sue Kinser, Diana Lissauer, Tim and Nina Zagat, Michael Trapp, Mary Byrne, Peter Trapp, Sally Pettus, Sandy Starkman, Victoria Love, John Dwyer, Doris Seidlitz, Moisha Blechman, Naga Antiques, and many friends in France. For additional photography, I am grateful to Christian and Ines Sarramon, who gave me carte blanche to their extraordinary archives, as well as to Michael Skott, Doyle's, and Sotheby's.

PHOTOGRAPHY CREDITS

All the photographs in this book are by Diane Love with the exception of:

Christian Sarramon: p.14; p.18; p.19: top and bottom left, top right; p. 20; p. 23; p. 25; p. 27; p. 29: all except #6; p. 30; p. 33; p. 35; p. 51: top right; p. 54: top and bottom left, top right; p. 58; p. 60; p. 64; p. 70: top and bottom right; p. 72; p. 76; p. 84: top left, top and bottom right; p. 86: top; p. 87: top; p. 88: top; p. 90: top; p. 94: top left and right; p. 95: top, middle, bottom left and top, middle right; p. 96: top, middle, and bottom left, top right; p. 97: bottom left, middle and bottom right; p.102: bottom left; p.112; p.114: top; p.116; p.120; p.123; p.125; p.126: bottom left; p.129; p. 132 : top left, top and bottom right; p.135; p.137; p.138: top right; p.140; p.144; p.147; p.149; p.150: bottom right.

Brad Calcaterra: p. 6, portrait at middle left.

Doyle's: p. 38: top ©1996; pps. 40–41: top©1998, middle©1997, bottom©1998; p.42: Adams©1998, Victorian©1998, Louis XVI©1995, Neoclassical©1998, Arts & Crafts©1998, Danish Modern©1998, Regency©1998, Empire©1996, Shaker©1997; p.43 Art Nouveau©1998, Queen Anne©1998, Bentwood©1998, Postmodern©1998, Bauhaus©1998.

Scott Frances: p. 8.

Michael Skott: p. 6: bottom left and middle right; p.10; p. 46: top left, top right; p. 47: top left and right; p. 49: top and bottom right; p. 50: top left, bottom right; p. 51: bottom left; p. 52: bottom left; p. 88: bottom; pps. 90–91; p. 97: top left; p.105; p.114: bottom; p.126: top right; p. 131; p. 138: top left.

Sotheby's: p. 38: bottom right © 1998; p. 42: Art Deco©1998.

CIP 99 075984

ISBN 0-8478-2300-8

First published in the United States of America in 2000
by Rizzoli International Publications, Inc.,
300 Park Avenue South, New York, NY 10010.

First published in France in 1999 by Flammarion, 26,
rue Racine, 75278 Paris.
Copyright © 1999 Flammarion

Text copyright © Diane Love

Printed and bound in France.

www.YESNODESIGN.com